Lives in Cricket

Michael Falcon
Norfolk's Gentleman Cricketer

Stephen Musk

With a foreword by David Armstrong

First published in Great Britain by
Association of Cricket Statisticians and Historians
Cardiff CF11 9XR
© ACS, 2010

British Library Cataloguing-in-Publication Data.
A catalogue record for this book is available from the British Library.

ISBN: 978 1 905138 88 3
Typeset by Limlow Books

Contents

Foreword   5

Introduction: East Anglia and Cricket   7

Chapter One: Early Life in Norfolk, and Harrow   10

Chapter Two: Varsity Days   17

Chapter Three: Taking Over the Reins at Norfolk: 1911–1914   25

Chapter Four: At Westminster   43

Chapter Five: At His Peak: 1919–1929   56

Chapter Six: Elder Statesman: 1930–1939   82

Chapter Seven: Second World War and Beyond   101

Chapter Eight: Life After Big-Time Cricket   108

Chapter Nine: A Test Cricketer?   115

Chapter Ten: Michael Falcon's Legacy   123

Acknowledgements   131

Bibliography   133

Appendix: Some Statistics   137

Index   144

Michael Falcon, as a Cambridge University player, in 1908.

Foreword
by David Armstrong

It gives me particular pleasure to write a foreword to Stephen Musk's account of the cricketing and many other facets of Michael Falcon's life, for I owe a huge debt of gratitude to a very great gentleman whose idea it was, over 43 years ago, to ask me to become Honorary Secretary of Norfolk County Cricket Club. His call set the course of my life through to retirement and, indeed, beyond.

If I may go back a few years further, I would nominate 1955 as a year of outstanding importance in my life. It was, sadly, the year my father died and (World Wars apart) the first cricket season since 1893 in which he had not been a part of Norfolk's cricketing following. This was particularly disappointing in that, after a succession of post-war seasons of false dawns, watching Norfolk had at last seen expectation overtake hope. This was also, as Stephen reports, the year in which was held a match at Lakenham for Geoff Edrich's Benefit, and this, in its turn, provided my first and only opportunity of watching Michael Falcon in action on the cricket field. Stephen gives the bare details of an economical spell of eight or so overs (delivered at a brisk medium pace) and of an undefeated innings of 37. I recall also a well-taken catch, above his head in the covers, which caused no trouble at all for that particular 67-year-old fielder. Stephen gently chides me for conferring on Bill Edrich, who dominated the day's proceedings, 'legendary' status. No slight was intended on my part, for to me Michael Falcon was more than a legend; but to my regret, he was a figure whose feats I could enjoy only vicariously.

Some years ago, I was telephoned by a well-known Minor County batsman – not a Norfolk man – to ask if he had overtaken Michael Falcon's batting aggregate. Answering that he had indeed achieved this target, I suggested that he now made a start on the 727 wickets!

To deal merely with statistics is to omit the quality of loyalty which, these days, is such a rarity both on the field of play and in committee rooms. Players and administrators alike seem nowadays to have but a tenuous connection with the team or club they serve and to move about as personal ambition, money and celebrity status dictate. To read of one whose efforts, all unpaid, were devoted to the county of his birth, should provide a lesson to us all.

I remember, with gratitude, a charming man buying a scorecard at Lakenham for my recently wedded wife and insisting on her accompanying him to the middle to be shown the length where Sydney Barnes was wont to wear a bare patch in the turf!

Thank you, Stephen, for your scholarly research; I am sure I shall not be the only person to have read your fascinating account in a single sitting.

Ridlington, Norfolk
February, 2010

Editor's Note: David Armstrong is very modest, both on his own behalf and about his father, Rev H.B.J.Armstrong, whose parish was at St James, Pockthorpe, and who was, according to the subject of this book, 'a mine of information' on 'the history of Norfolk cricket' and an accomplished raconteur in the enclosure at Lakenham, Norfolk's home ground between 1881 and 2000. As for his son, David not only served the Norfolk County Club loyally and efficiently on the Committee for many years, but he also became Honorary Secretary of the Minor Counties Cricket Association between 1983 and 1985, and Secretary from 1985 until 2001. This was no sinecure for, especially towards the end of his period in office, it was a time of great change in the Minor Counties game. David helped to oversee the experiment with 'grade' cricket and, though he retired just before the adoption of the three-day format which has proved to be such an outstanding success, his patient spadework undoubtedly aided the transition to the longer game (of which more in Chapter Six). As passionate a spectator as his father, David has seen Norfolk play away games at nearly one hundred different grounds across the country.

Introduction
East Anglia and Cricket

Early Saxon England was divided into numerous petty kingdoms with each struggling for pre-eminence. The most influential king at any time was given the title of Bretwalda. In the early seventh century the Bretwalda was Raedwald, who was leader of the kingdom of the East Angles (which stretched over the modern counties of Suffolk, Norfolk and Essex) and was a member of the Wuffinga dynasty. After he died, the power of his successors waned and East Anglia lost its political supremacy, never to regain it. The kingdom was already in decline before the destructive raids of the Vikings led to chaos and upheaval.

When East Anglia was restored to Saxon rule, the region prospered again. In late Saxon and early Norman England, Norwich was one of the largest towns in the kingdom and the rural economy was booming. Some evidence of this is found in the presence of large numbers of round-tower churches in the county of Norfolk. More evidence is found in the Domesday Book, which reveals the region to be an economic powerhouse. Norwich became even more important, meriting a fine cathedral.

The existence of over sixty medieval churches in Norwich attests to its continuing prosperity and its position at the heart of the most productive arable land in the country contributed to its growth so that, between the sixteenth and early eighteenth centuries, Norwich was the second largest city in the kingdom. East Anglian agriculture was genuinely innovative as the development of the 'Norfolk rotation' method of farming was invented. Then, however, the Industrial Revolution took place and East Anglia as a whole, lacking in the relevant raw materials, began to fall behind. Norfolk's geographic isolation also told against it and the county became a rural backwater as quickly as the early nineteenth century. Whilst the county town can boast of the 'Norwich School' of painting, the choice facing most people of talent and ambition was clear: in order to achieve success you had to leave Norfolk and follow the money.

This fact of life applied to cricketers as much as any other trade. Norfolk has produced many fine cricketers but most have moved on from their county of birth in order to further their ambition. The first was Fuller Pilch, easily Norfolk's most skilful player in the 1830s, who was lured away to Kent in 1836 by an offer of £100 per annum, leaving behind a virtual vacuum. Similarly, Bill Edrich, a highly talented all-rounder a century later, qualified for Middlesex and went on to play Test cricket with considerable success. His cousin, John Edrich, moved to Surrey and also had a prolific Test career. Others whose transfers away from Norfolk led to international recognition were Peter Parfitt, Clive Radley and Martin Saggers, whilst several more emigrants have played first-class county cricket.

In the face of this efflux, two cricketers who have every right to be considered amongst the best ever born in Norfolk have bucked the trend. They turned their backs on fame and fortune, preferring instead to play for Norfolk and for fun. One was David Walker, an immensely talented batsman, who scored nearly 4,000 Minor Counties Championship runs at an average of over 60 and who turned down approaches to play first-class cricket with Leicestershire, Middlesex, Sussex and Surrey.[1] Walker's nine-year career, during which he played only sporadically, was terminated by the Second World War, in which he was tragically killed whilst on active service.

The other cricketer who stayed in Norfolk was even more important than David Walker. Michael Falcon made his debut for Norfolk against the 1906 West Indians whilst still a schoolboy and was an integral member of the side by the time he was appointed captain in 1912. From then, until say 1929 he was both the best batsman and the best bowler in the county side and, although age reduced his powers, he remained worth his place in the side until his last year as captain in 1946. His achievement of captaining his county before the First World War and after the Second is unique.

This biography aims to chart the deeds of Michael Falcon, both as a Norfolk cricketer and on the first-class scene, where he represented Cambridge University, the Gentlemen and the Free

---

[1]   According to Bill Edrich – who was writing to Walker's godson – the Norfolk opening bat was 'with the possible exception of Don Bradman ... the best batsman in the world!' I am indebted to Andy Archer, a disc jockey with BBC Radio Norfolk, who has conducted some preliminary research for a biography of David Walker, for this information.

Foresters amongst others. His successes in his occasional appearances in the first-class arena have led many well-informed observers of the game to suggest that, had he had the inclination, he could have played Test cricket. That he didn't play on the international stage didn't bother him in the slightest: he would rather play for Norfolk.

As this record shows, Michael Falcon was born at Horstead, just north of Norwich, and thus qualified to play for Norfolk by birth.

Chapter One
Early Life in Norfolk, and Harrow

Michael Falcon, the famous Norfolk cricketer, was born on 21 July 1888, at Horstead House, in the village of Horstead, now not far from Norwich Airport, on the northern edge of the city.[2] His father was also named Michael Falcon and was in turn the son of another Michael Falcon. The grandfather lived in Stainburn, near Workington in Cumberland, where he was a magistrate: his son was born on 28 June 1859. The son's wife was Isabella Mordy,[3] daughter of William Mordy of Workington: they married on 13 April 1886 and had four children – Isabella, Michael, William and Joseph Henry (commonly known as Harry). The father, who from now on will be referred to as Michael Falcon senior, was educated at Repton School, but did not go to university. Instead he studied at the Royal Agricultural College at Cirencester.

Moving to Norfolk, Michael Falcon senior put his training to good use by becoming a land agent. He soon had a flourishing practice, being appointed to manage some of the largest estates in Norfolk, such as Blickling Hall which he ran from 1890 to 1920. He founded the firm of Falcon and Birkbeck with Christopher Birkbeck (originally from Ripon), based at Horstead House, where he had settled in 1881, renting the property from Vice-Admiral John Corbett (later Admiral Sir John). Made a Fellow of the Institution of Surveyors, Michael Falcon senior became involved with the Norwich Union Building Society in due course. He was elected a director of the NU Life Insurance Society in 1906, later visiting

---

2   The 1891 Census records a household of eleven at Horstead House, including six live-in servants. The building is described these days by English Heritage as 'a former manor house, dating from 1620, with eighteenth- and nineteenth-century alterations and additions'. It is now owned by Matthew Fleming, who played for Kent from 1988 to 2002 and for England in eleven limited-overs internationals in 1997 and 1998. Falcon's birthplace is sometimes erroneously given as Sprowston Hall, a residence acquired by his father in 1925.

3   Both Falcon and Mordy are, if not common names in Cumberland, then at least relatively more frequent there than anywhere else in Great Britain. Falcon originated as a nickname referring to the bird and its characteristics. Hawke is similarly said to be a nickname indicating 'a person of savage or cruel disposition'. Falcon and Lord Hawke are the longest-serving captains in, respectively, Minor Counties and first-class county cricket.

Falcon's birthplace, Horstead House, on a bright day in 2009.

Cricket being played at the Suffield Park preparatory school, Cromer, in Falcon's time there. It is not known whether he was present at this match.

South Africa on its behalf. In 1928 he was elected vice-president and, two years later, became president, retiring from this post in 1936. In parallel, he had been elected a director of the NU Fire Insurance Society in 1915, being elected vice-chairman in 1929 and chairman in 1930.

Michael Falcon senior was a churchwarden of Horstead Parish Church and, having served as a magistrate, like his father, was appointed High Sheriff of Norfolk in 1925.[4] Until disabled by failing eyesight, he was a very fine shot and a keen fisherman: for many years he travelled to Scotland and Norway, inviting friends to join him in his hunting activities. In summary, he was a successful businessman of impeccable reputation and a fine role model for his three sons, all of whom were educated at Harrow School. Whilst there was thus a family tradition of public service which his oldest son would more than live up to, there was nothing to suggest that young Michael would become one of the finest amateur fast bowlers in England.

Before Michael Falcon moved on to Harrow, he attended Gordon Winter's Suffield Park Boys' School in Cromer, and he was recorded there by the census of 1901. Unfortunately no details of his stay on the north Norfolk coast remain, and, outside of cricket, little is known of his time at Harrow, where the school archive was not established until 1981. What remains informs us that he was a member of Rendalls House,[5] that he was a monitor in his final year in 1907, and that he played in the school's football first team in 1906. His son, Michael Gascoigne, remembers that his father won a trophy for finishing first in a four-mile cross-country run.

Michael Falcon first steps into the spotlight as a cricketer when appearing in the 1906 and 1907 fixtures against Eton at Lord's. Immediately one runs into the almost universally held misconception about his career: that he started off as a batsman who subsequently developed into a bowler (in the first-class game) or an all-rounder (in the Minor County game). The Cambridge University averages from 1908 to 1911 indeed reveal that he bowled little until his final year, in which he was the leading wicket-taker, as well as topping the batting averages. Similarly,

---

4   The office of High Sheriff, once an important one in the administration of justice, was by this time largely, if not entirely, ceremonial in nature. Being elected High Sheriff constituted a recognition that an individual had undertaken a substantial body of work on behalf of the public good.

5   Rendalls later boasted the actors Edward and James Fox among its notable members.

inspection of the Norfolk averages reveals that Falcon did not become a bowler of note until 1910. However, if Michael Falcon's own account of his first-ever important match, published in Bernard Darwin's *Eton v Harrow at Lord's*, is to be believed, he approached his Lord's debut against Eton expecting to be a specialist strike bowler.

'Together join'd in cricket's manly toil', the Harrow School side of 1906.
Back row (l to r): B.Osborne, A.W.M.S.Griffin, D.R.Brandt (wk), J.B.Royle,
H.E.C.Biedermann.
Seated: M.Falcon, R.E.Eiloart, E.H.Crake (capt), M.C.Bird, A.H.Lang.
On the ground: G.A.Laverton.
Five of this side played first-class cricket in their time, but they lost to Eton at
Lord's by four wickets.

Unfortunately for the Harrow XI, batsman Clive Reunert fractured his finger in the run-up to the big match and Michael Falcon, who had been given his 'flannels' early in the season for his feats as a right-arm paceman and who was accustomed to bat at nine or ten, was promoted to bat at number four. Harrow won the toss and batted first, but did not take full advantage, being dismissed for 230. When Eton went in to reply, Falcon opened the bowling but was completely ineffective, beginning with a wide and failing to improve much: eventually he sent down 25 wicketless overs for 52 runs as Eton built up a lead of 135. In Harrow's second innings

Falcon (who batted like he bowled, right-handed) played pluckily, if not faultlessly, for a top score of 79 before being run out. Three more wicketless overs in Eton's victorious run-chase left him looking more like a batsman than a bowler and he finished the school season with a creditable batting average of 25.50.

Those in charge of Norfolk cricket took note of Falcon's innings and offered him a place in their eleven to play the touring West Indians at Lakenham. Batting again at number four, he made an inauspicious start to what would turn out to be a forty-year career for Norfolk by making a duck in the first innings and only five in his second knock as Norfolk followed on and lost by an innings and 118 runs. Michael Falcon did at least earn his first favourable review in the *Eastern Daily Press*, lasting long enough in his innings of five for the paper to say that he 'batted in promising style'.

He had a disappointing season playing for Harrow in 1907, failing to push on from the form of the previous year. He did nothing of note against Eton with the bat, failing to reach double figures despite opening the batting, although he did take three wickets as a change bowler.[6] The highlight of his season was an innings of 61 against the tourists from Pennsylvania University, but his batting average dropped to 19.25. That the inveterate compiler of XIs, E.H.D.Sewell, included him in his all-time Harrow side, when writing in 1943, was probably due to the feats that Falcon would later achieve rather than his performances as a schoolboy as such.[7]

It was for Norfolk in 1907 that Michael Falcon's cricketing talent really came to public attention for the first time. In the four matches in which he played, he amassed 458 runs at an average of 76.33, including three centuries; 110 against Bedfordshire, 112 against Cambridgeshire and an unbeaten 102 against Harrow Wanderers, all made in a period of seven days. The *Eastern Daily Press* commented, several times, that he had a wide range of attacking strokes.

---

6   At this point the player in the Harrow team who looked the most promising was Morice Bird, who scored two centuries (one unbeaten) against Eton in 1907 - a feat never equalled in the history of this fixture. On the basis of his early promise, he played in ten Tests before the Great War, but with little impact, and he finished with first-class figures inferior to those of Falcon. He served at Gallipoli and was invalided out of the Army in 1916; he played little after the War and died young.

7   Sewell had Falcon down to bat at nine and so was obviously considering him to be a bowler: as has been described, however, Falcon's impact as a bowler for Harrow in big games was minimal. Lt-Col Hon Gerald French, like Sewell something of an oddball, put him as a bowler in an all-time Harrow Wanderers side which he published in 1948.

Of passing interest is a friendly match played at Lakenham on 5 September 1907, between M.Falcon's XI and the Rev Morgan's XI. It is the only surviving recorded occasion on which all three Falcon brothers played on the same team – Harry played quite a bit for Norfolk, but it is the only traceable match featuring William Falcon outside of his appearances for Harrow. Michael Falcon dominated with the bat, retiring for 126 out of a total of only 211, whilst William contributed 23 and Harry 21. The retirement was shown to be premature as Morgan's side replied with 258 for five, future Norfolk batsman Ralph Thurgar making 116. Michael Falcon took two wickets, his brothers one each.

This is perhaps a point in the story where we should say a little more of Michael's siblings. Harry Falcon followed his elder brother from Harrow to Pembroke College, Cambridge but, despite showing some promise in Harrow's match against Eton in 1911, he failed to establish himself in the Cambridge University XI. He played only two first-class games, both in 1914, remaining undefeated with the bat and claiming five wickets with his fast-medium bowling. Sadly, he did not obtain a degree, failing both to meet the residence requirements and to sit all the requisite examinations. He played sporadically for Norfolk between 1910 and 1924, mostly under the captaincy of his brother, with little success either as a batsman or as a bowler. His one day in the sun was in a fixture against Essex II at Witham in 1920 when he made an unbeaten 103, his only score above 50. Even then he was trumped by his brother, who made 134 in the same innings and then took six wickets when Essex batted. As a cricketer, Harry remained thoroughly overshadowed by Michael's deeds on the cricket pitch and it was only in the Army, where he outranked his elder brother, that he shone in his own right. Harry took a Danish wife called Greta; they had no offspring and he died in 1950, at the comparatively early age of 57, whilst living in Lowestoft.

Ironically it was William, the one brother who did not go on to play cricket at a significant standard after leaving school, who put in the most impressive performance when playing for Harrow against Eton. In 1909 he returned figures of 12-5-17-4 as Eton were dismissed for 92, conceding a first-innings deficit of 43. However, Harrow collapsed in turn for 76 in the second innings and Eton went on to win by three wickets, William Falcon being strangely underused in Eton's run chase. He did not go to university, but studied mining in South Wales before the Great War. He was granted probate of his father's will along with his mother and brother Michael, in 1939, at which point he was living in Devon. William married Louise Carter-Jonas and had three children. He passed away in 1970.

Sister Isabella married John Habgood in 1915 and, like William, had three children, one of whom, John Michael (known as Johnny), survived Dunkirk and won an MC at Tobruk. Johnny in turn was the father of Anthony Habgood, who became chairman of the Whitbread brewing concern. John Habgood (senior) was active in local politics, being an activist for the Conservative Party in eastern Norfolk in the 1920s and 1930s.

Chapter Two
Varsity Days

In the 1908 edition of *Wisden*, Michael Falcon was listed as one of thirty cricketers going up to Cambridge University. Falcon did indeed study at Cambridge, going to Pembroke College in the autumn of 1907, thereby following a long line of Old Harrovians. Matriculating on 21 October, he went up intending to read for honours in law, with the object of making his living as a barrister. For the first two years of his undergraduate course he resided at 25 Fitzwilliam Street, near to his college. Little is known of his deeds in Cambridge off the cricket pitch, but it was cricket that was his true *raison d'etre* for being at Cambridge.

1908

No scorebooks survive which relate to Pembroke College cricket at this period, but some information of college matches filtered back to Norfolk to appear in the local press. Falcon would clearly have had his eye on higher honours than college cricket from the start. His record as a batsman for Harrow was solid, if unspectacular, but his successes for Norfolk in 1907 suggested that he had the talent to make his mark at the University level. Success was not guaranteed however and he had first to impress in the Freshmen's Match in order to gain a place in the Eleven, and then impress still further in order to obtain his Blue. Prior to this important match he did manage to fit in a couple of games for Pembroke, in order to get his eye in, but in neither did his score go beyond the twenties so he couldn't really be said to have been in form.

However, Michael Falcon did indeed make runs in the Freshmen's Match, scoring 86 and 10 for R.A.Young's side against C.C.G.Wright's side, and as a result he made his first-class debut for Cambridge University against Lancashire at Fenner's on 25 May 1908. He did little of note, scoring 11 and 18 in a heavy defeat. Further unsuccessful appearances followed and, according to the *Manchester Guardian*, he would have lost his place in the side to play Sussex if John Ireland had been able to play. Falcon made the

The Cambridge University side of 1908, in Falcon's freshman season.
Standing (l to r): Hon C.F.Lyttelton, R.E.H.Baily (wk), K.G.MacLeod, E.Olivier.
Seated: F.H.Mugliston, J.N.Buchanan, R.A.Young (capt), C.C.G.Wright,
H.J.Goodwin.
On the ground: J.F.Ireland, M.Falcon.

The Norfolk side of 1908, with Falcon now in his third year of Minor County
cricket.
Standing (l to r): T.H.Wharton, George Stevens, G.A.Stevens (wk), M.Falcon.
Seated: O.H.C.Dunell, B.Cozens-Hardy, L.Barratt (capt), J.N.Worman,
A.K.Watson.
On the ground: C.E.Dunning, E.Gibson.

most of his chance, making 44 in the first innings and 60 in the second. In the first innings he played second fiddle to Cyril Wright, helping him put on 123 runs for the fifth wicket, but in his second knock, he played a lone hand, batting for two hours before being last out. Both the *Manchester Guardian* and the *Daily Telegraph* praised his 60, whilst noting that he was missed in the slips before he had opened his account, but *The Times* was less enthusiastic about his stand with Wright, stating that neither played particularly well.

Falcon went on to play steady innings against Surrey and in a return game with Sussex which earned him mixed reviews. *The Times* reported that a tedious innings of 37 in 110 minutes earned him some ironical applause, but the *Manchester Guardian* described his batting as 'cool and restrained' and his scoring strokes were referred to as 'well-made without being wholly conventional in the sense of the average public-school coach'. This doesn't seem like unconditional praise, but the paper leavened this with the news that he had been awarded his Blue. The highlight of the University season for Michael Falcon came in the return fixture with MCC at Lord's. The *Daily Telegraph*, like the magazine *Cricket,* disagreed with the *Guardian,* dated the award of his Blue to this match and reported that he started nervously but improved greatly later on, hitting very cleanly and confidently in his innings of 122. *The Times* observed fine drives and leg-glances in an admirable innings whilst the *Manchester Guardian* – describing Falcon as the 'most dependable bat on the side' – made the first of what were to become many references to his driving on both sides of the wicket. He hit 15 fours in an innings of two hours 15 minutes which led to a two-wicket victory.

Michael Falcon did little in the Varsity Match but finished a satisfactory second in the Cambridge University batting list with an average of 30.22. He was asked to do little with the ball for the University but it is of significance that, when he was rested for the match against Yorkshire, he played in an inter-college game in which he took five wickets for 20 runs. Clearly the urge to bowl was still with him, even if it wasn't being expressed at the highest level. Unfortunately for Norfolk's supporters he was unable to continue his form into the Minor Counties season: in six matches he amassed a mere 147 runs, including 54 against Cambridgeshire. A 'pair' against Bedfordshire helped ensure it was the worst season he ever experienced with the bat for Norfolk.

1909

Michael Falcon continued to live in Fitzwilliam Street in his second year at Pembroke and fulfilled his academic commitments before starting his cricket season, achieving a third-class mark in the Law Tripos Part I. The University played fewer first-class matches than in the previous season; Falcon played in six out of the seven and continued to impress with the bat. The highlight of his season was his first contest in a first-class fixture against a touring side, the 1909 Australians. The tourists thoroughly dominated the match; the University, having to follow on, were saved from defeat by inclement weather. Few of the Cambridge batsmen did anything but Falcon was an exception, top-scoring in the first innings with 46. *The Times*, not always a fan of Michael Falcon's batting in his early days, noted some excellent leg-side strokes and some 'dogged' resistance while the *Daily Telegraph* described his innings as 'well-judged'.

Statistically, Falcon's best performance of the University season was his innings of 130 against Sussex, but he was lucky in that he was dropped three times. Also noteworthy was a partnership of 51 with John Ireland in the Varsity match, which the *Daily Telegraph* described as a 'delightful exhibition of batting' and which allowed Cambridge to hold out for a draw. For the second year running, Michael Falcon averaged over 30 and was placed second in the Cambridge batting lists.

For some reason, lost now in the mists of time, Falcon did not turn out at all for Norfolk in 1909, and he was also conspicuous by his absence from an otherwise well-attended meeting held at the end of the cricket season in order to discuss the future of Norfolk county cricket. At the start of the University season, the local press were expecting Falcon to turn out for his home county, and furthermore, they were expecting his Pembroke team-mate, Frank Mann, to play as well. (Mann was the son of Sir Edward Mann of Thelveton and thus had a residential qualification to play for Norfolk.) Whatever he was doing, Falcon does not seem to have been busy playing in high-quality social cricket elsewhere in the country.

1910

In his final year as an undergraduate, Michael Falcon was resident in Pembroke College, on K staircase in Ivy Court. His appointment to the captaincy of Cambridge University in 1910 was not unexpected, given his record for Cambridge and for Norfolk in the preceding two years. At the beginning of the cricket season he had to juggle his sporting commitments with the necessity of revising for his finals; three of the University's nine first-class fixtures took place before his Part II examinations, with the game against Kent finishing the day before the start of those examinations. (These took place at the Law Schools between 2 and 4 June.) He was again awarded a third-class mark in the Law Tripos Part II – like two-thirds of the other candidates in this particular subject – and was placed equal 27th in the class list.

After a few days' rest, Falcon returned to his duties as captain and one of the leading batsmen of the Cambridge side. However, although there were a couple of highlights with the bat, his form dropped significantly from the previous two years. He had done little before his examinations, but finally found some form against Yorkshire, top-scoring with 63 after Lord Hawke put Cambridge in. Despite being hit in the face, Falcon hit 10 fours as the University batted consistently and rapidly. In reply, Yorkshire collapsed and Falcon enforced the follow-on. In their second innings, George Hirst reached an unbeaten 141 by close-of-play on the second day and both the *Manchester Guardian* and *The Times* questioned Falcon's decision not to bat again. However, the Yorkshire second innings was swiftly wrapped up on the final day and the final margin of nine wickets vindicated the skipper's decision. The victory over the white rose county was probably the highlight of Michael Falcon's captaincy of Cambridge University.

Later in the term, a Gentlemen's XI was also made to follow on. They scored over 400 runs at their second attempt, to set Cambridge a sizeable total. Promoting himself to open the batting, Falcon made 96 in the successful run chase, giving what the *Daily Telegraph* described as a 'splendid display'. He hit 18 fours in an innings of 105 minutes, his driving coming in for special praise. *The Times* also lauded his driving on both sides of the wicket, but the *Manchester Guardian* stated that the Gentlemen's bowling attack was not strong.

The Varsity Match started well, despite Falcon losing the toss, but soon fortunes turned. The fast but erratic Alexander Cowie dismissed two batsmen in the first over and Oxford were soon 30 for four. At this point Philip Le Couteur came in to join Charles Hooman in a century stand. After the latter was dismissed for 61, Le Couteur totally dominated proceedings. He went on to make 160 out of 315 and then took six for 20 and five for 46 with his leg-spinners on a helpfully wet pitch as Cambridge went down by an innings. *The Times* made scathing remarks about Cambridge's bowling and fielding, but the truth is they were beaten by a virtuoso one-man performance unique in the history of Cambridge *v* Oxford contests: no-one else has done the match-double of a century and ten wickets.[8] What was supposed to be the climax of his University cricket career was thus a sad disappointment for Michael Falcon.

In contrast to 1909, Falcon (who had dropped to fifth place in the Cambridge batting list with an average of 22.86) turned out no fewer than nine times for title-winning Norfolk in the 1910 Minor Counties season, which culminated in the Challenge Match against Berkshire. He was so enthusiastic to play for Norfolk that, finding himself touring Ireland with Cambridge University and short of time, he crossed the Irish Sea overnight and travelled cross-country in the small hours of the morning in order to turn out against Bedfordshire. The season was dominated by the performances of Norfolk's veteran skipper Rev George Raikes, whose main claim to sporting fame was that he played as England's goalkeeper at association football. Raikes played in eight games, winning seven outright and achieving a first-innings lead in the drawn game. He scored 679 runs at 61.72 and took 57 wickets at 10.66: in every match in which he played he had a significant impact on the result, even in the Challenge Match in which Geoffrey Stevens' innings of 201 has tended to obscure all other contributions. Falcon had modest success with the bat, scoring just over 300 runs with three fifties, but the remarkable feature of his season was his sudden reappearance as a strike bowler.

---

8   Philip Le Couteur was a Rhodes Scholar from Australia whose first-class career was almost entirely limited to his three years at Oxford (1909-1911). He was considered promising enough to represent the Gentlemen six times and, at The Oval in 1911, his bowling was largely responsible for the Gentlemen achieving a rare win. He returned to Australia, but played only three games for Victoria before dropping out of first-class cricket. He became a lecturer in philosophy at the University of Western Australia, where he still holds several all-rounders' records.

He delivered more than 200 overs and took 39 wickets at an average of just over 17. His best return was seven for 53 against Nottinghamshire II, where the *Eastern Daily Press* reported that he 'bowled at a good pace'. There was also evidence of both pace and swing when he took five wickets against Bedfordshire. *Cricket* magazine also described Falcon's bowling as fast and, in addition, noted the existence of a slower ball. His fielding was also lauded; he was described as being 'very prominent for fine work' in the Challenge Match, whilst the *Eastern Daily Press* described him as a genuine all-rounder, saying that 'his value to the side did not rest solely upon his batting. He saved scores of runs in the field, and he was also worth playing for his fast bowling alone.' The sudden emergence of Falcon as a strike bowler who was more or less the finished article is remarkable.

There were also signs that, although he was still only 22 years of age, Michael Falcon was already being groomed for the captaincy once Raikes retired. The latter was late arriving for the home fixture with Nottinghamshire II and it was Falcon who tossed in his

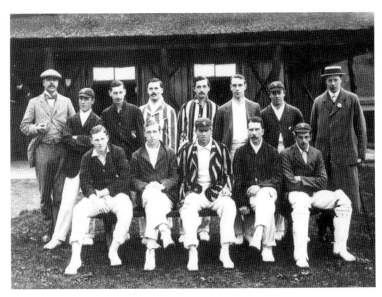

Norfolk's championship-winning side of 1910, at Lakenham for their successful match with Nottinghamshire II in early August.
Standing (l to r): B.K.Wilson (hon sec), E.Gibson, E.J.Fulcher, G.Williams, G.W.Birkbeck, R.W.Collinson, T.C.Allsopp, C.B.L.Prior (hon sec).
Seated: G.A.Stevens, M.Falcon, Rev G.B.Raikes (capt), R.A.A.Beresford, R.W.Thurgar (wk).

absence – he lost. He also captained Norfolk in their friendly against MCC, a match which was lost due to a fine innings of 140 by Len Braund.

Thus, 1910 was the first year of what might be described as a 'Golden Age' of Norfolk cricket. Between then and the onset of the First World War, Norfolk won the Minor Counties Championship twice and reached an undecided final on a third occasion, as can be seen in Chapter Three.

Chapter Three

Taking Over the Reins at Norfolk: 1911-1914

At the end of the 1910 cricket season Michael Falcon underwent the ceremonial niceties that would enable him to practise as a barrister, graduating in both B.A. and LL.B. (Bachelor of Law) on 13 October. In November 1911, he was called to the Bar by the Inner Temple, the most prestigious of the four Inns of Court, and joined the South-Eastern judiciary circuit. He continued to practise until the Great War from chambers at 6 Crown Office Row in the Temple, while living at Cadogan Terrace, just off Sloane Square. His son recalls that there was sometimes a certain levity in his cases in that his University cronies would turn up to support him: the public gallery would be a centre of high spirits and laughter. On one unfortunate occasion for Falcon he found himself referring to a damaged item of ladies' underwear which led to absolute uproar from the supporters' club. Among the worst 'offenders' was Frank Mann, a future England captain. Mann and Falcon were particularly close friends whose families remained in contact for decades; Manns and Falcons frequently acted as godparents to each others' children.

Falcon as a young barrister.

Falcon was now entering upon his own personal 'Golden Age' of cricket, a period terminated only by the onset of the First World War, and coinciding with a similar 'Golden Age' for Norfolk cricket as a whole, referred to earlier. Playing for Norfolk from now on as a genuine all-rounder, he was to take over the captaincy from Raikes in 1912 and lead the county to further successes.[9] Good performances in a smattering of first-class games kept his bowling in the public eye and he was rewarded with several invitations to represent the Gentlemen against the Players.

1911

Although he had graduated from Cambridge in 1910, regulations permitted Michael Falcon to play for the University for one more season. It proved to be his best year for Cambridge. Not only did he top the batting averages but, after a slow start, he showed that his bowling for Norfolk in the previous season had not been a fluke by spearheading the University attack and becoming its leading wicket-taker. For the only time in his first-class career he had the credentials (and the averages) of a genuine all-rounder and he was a cricketer of real promise, a fact recognised by the invitation to represent the Gentlemen at Scarborough. Although it is impossible to date, it was probably at around this time that Falcon was approached to qualify for Middlesex by Frank Mann and 'Plum' Warner and turned them down, preferring to represent his home county.

His first performance of note for Cambridge was an innings of 134 – his career-best in first-class cricket, marked by 'clean, hard hitting' in all directions – against Sussex which set up a victory by 41 runs after the University had been invited to follow on. In the absence of skipper John Ireland, Falcon was acting as captain, and it is a sign of how slowly that his bowling became established as an integral part of the Cambridge attack that he gave himself only eight overs in the whole match. Taking a break from University cricket, Falcon represented MCC against Leicestershire and was again successful, scoring 115. This was his fourth first-class century and turned out to be his last, although no-one would have been able to foresee that at the time.

---

9   In the 20 games in which Falcon skippered Norfolk before the Great War, he led them to 11 outright victories and first-innings points in six of the eight drawn games. Norfolk's only reverse came at Stoke where Sydney Barnes' match haul of 12 for 61 was largely responsible for an innings defeat. Falcon dismissed Barnes for a duck when Staffordshire batted, but the compliment was returned when Falcon opened Norfolk's follow-on.

Falcon's breakthrough with the ball occurred against the Indian tourists. When they followed on Falcon returned figures of five for 50, helping to dismiss them for 180 and inflicting upon them an innings defeat. It was his first five-wicket haul in first-class cricket, but there would be 19 more in his brief first-class career. He was also successful in his next match, an innings defeat at the hands of Surrey. In the Cambridge second innings, only Falcon, with an unbeaten 70, and skipper Ireland, with 59, reached double figures. Falcon's good form continued against Sussex; when the county were set only 91 to win, he bowled finely and was largely responsible for their collapse to 61 for nine. However, Bertie Chaplin and Henry Roberts managed to knock off the runs for victory and Falcon had to be content with figures of five for 40. Further success followed against MCC, who were defeated by an innings. He scored 65 and took three for 32 and five for 25, his bowling being difficult to play on a rain-affected pitch.

Falcon's figures against Oxford didn't really do him justice, but the *Daily Telegraph* and the *Guardian* both praised his bowling whilst the often-hostile *Times* employed the word 'brilliance' of his performance. Cambridge lost again but Falcon had done enough to earn an invitation to play for the Gentlemen at Scarborough at the season's end.[10] Given the new ball he rapidly fired out Wilfred Rhodes and Johnny Tyldesley and later came back to dismiss Phil Mead, albeit after Mead had compiled a double century, finishing with figures of three for 87. The Gentlemen collapsed before the bowling of Frank Field, who took the first six wickets to fall: at this point, with the score on 64, Falcon joined Bernard Bosanquet. They put on 147 for the seventh wicket in 70 minutes, Falcon making 75 (which was to remain his highest score for the Gentlemen) and Bosanquet scoring 103. It was one of the better pieces of amateur batsmanship at the festival in the immediate pre-War years and probably Falcon's most impressive innings in first-class cricket.

Having won the Minor Counties Championship in 1910, Norfolk had high hopes for the 1911 season and employed ex-Test player Fred Tate as coach in the pre-season nets at Lakenham. Unfortunately things did not go according to plan and only the last two games were won. The problem was that in a fine, dry summer, the attack was unpenetrative, with Raikes, who finished top of the bowling averages, taking his wickets at the high cost, by Minor

---

10   His contemporaries among faster amateur bowlers included Walter Brearley, William Burns, Johnny Douglas and Frank Foster.

Counties' standards, of 20.39 runs apiece. Michael Falcon played in nine games, but a strain prevented him bowling in all these matches and his final return of 22 wickets was at 22.33 runs each. This was to be his most expensive season for Norfolk with the ball until 1929, when age was beginning to reduce his effectiveness: it was of note that his first-class bowling average for 1911 was lower than his Minor Counties bowling average. The strain was a collector's item: in a career of such a length as his, Falcon kept remarkably fit and free from injury.

In contrast to his poor performance with the ball for Norfolk, Michael Falcon did exceptionally well with the bat, scoring 631 runs with two centuries and four other scores above fifty. He made runs all round the ground but the feature of his batting was, as usual, his powerful driving on each side of the wicket. His achievement was, however, put in the shade by the batting of Geoffrey Stevens who made no fewer than 908 runs.[11]

Michael Falcon also found time to participate in an MCC tour to Norfolk, in which he showed that, at levels below the very highest, he was an extremely potent pace bowler indeed. Against Mid-Norfolk at East Dereham, he started with a devastating spell of five overs and one ball in which he took seven wickets for three runs (including a hat-trick) and was largely responsible for the locals' dismissal for a mere 11 runs. Although meeting stiffer resistance from a strong Overstrand team and from XII of Yarmouth and District, he still managed to add another 13 wickets to his bag, bowling all eight of his victims against Yarmouth. It was truly a case of a man against boys.

1912

The 1912 season promised much for Michael Falcon, before ending in a series of deluges which left Norfolk underwater and brought a soggy end to local cricket. This was the year of the triangular Test tournament which gave Falcon the chance to have his first crack as a bowler at both the Australians and the South Africans. However,

---

11   Geoffrey Stevens was one of Norfolk's all-time great batsmen. Like Falcon, he made his debut in 1906 (and like Falcon he started with a duck) and went on to score over 8,000 runs at an average of over 32 before retiring in 1930. He made two Championship double centuries and took 137 catches, mostly at first slip – where he was originally stationed in desperation, having proved inept in all other positions. Although he played but three first-class games with little success, David Armstrong's *Short History of Norfolk County Cricket* speaks of 'Test Trial claims' being made on his behalf, apparently by E.H.D.Sewell.

both touring teams were scheduled to visit Norfolk late in the year, and Falcon had to attend to the Minor Counties Championship first. With a fixture list of eight games, Norfolk, now led by Falcon, had an excellent season, winning seven matches and losing only one. Before Norfolk's final match (against Cambridgeshire) the secretary, C.B.L.Prior, wrote to his counterpart in Staffordshire asking him whether, if the two counties were to finish first and second in the table, Staffordshire (who were likely to finish second) would issue a challenge. The Staffordshire secretary, W.C.Hancock, replied that his county had not done well financially that year and to spend three days in Norfolk would be out of the question.

However, the scenario envisaged by Prior duly materialised and Staffordshire changed their minds, issuing a challenge on 31 August. By this time Norfolk was suffering from the worst floods in living memory[12] and Prior replied that 'owing to the flood disaster and the general distress in Norfolk' it would be impossible to meet the challenge. At first it seemed that Norfolk might have to forfeit the title, but when Dr J.Earl Norman, the secretary of the Minor Counties Association, and Hancock conferred and suggested to Prior that the Challenge Match should take place in Stoke, he reacted rapidly and convened a meeting of the Norfolk Committee. They proposed a match starting on 19 September, but the Staffordshire secretary replied that his county would be unable to play owing to the 'undue delay'. In the end the Championship was left 'in abeyance', a curiosity which still appears in record books.

Including friendlies, Michael Falcon played in nine out of the ten games, the secretary C.B.L.Prior being unable to tempt him away from the Harrow Wanderers' tour in order to play against Suffolk. He had a fine all-round season, topping the batting with over 500 runs and taking 38 wickets. This was the season when Norfolk's bowling was dominated by the debutant professional, Roderick Falconer, who had been performing well for Northamptonshire Club and Ground but who was qualified to play for Norfolk by birth. He had an amazing year, securing 65 wickets at 7.94 apiece,

---

12   A total of 11.27 inches of rain fell on Norwich in August, the city's wettest month ever, easily surpassing a previous record in the 'Great Norwich Flood' of November 1878. Rain fell on 27 days in August with 6.59 inches on 26 August and, unsurprisingly, there was chaos. All communications were suspended, rail services were cancelled and no fewer than 80 bridges failed across the county. The Falcon family contributed significantly to the Horstead Relief Fund.

The Norfolk side of 1912, when the title was held 'in abeyance'. This was the team for the home fixture against Cambridgeshire in mid-August.
Standing (l to r): E.Gibson, H.Watson, C.B.L.Prior (hon sec), R.W.Thurgar (wk), R.F.Popham, G.W.Birkbeck, L.F.Wynne-Wilson, R.Falconer.
Seated: E.J.Fulcher, G.A.Stevens, M.Falcon (capt), Rev G.B.Raikes, R.G.Pilch.

taking five wickets in an innings nine times and ten in a match thrice.[13] His team-mates bowled well in support, but it was Falconer who took most of the plaudits. Falcon's bowling was, however, praised in the press: he bowled at a 'terrific pace', at a 'great pace' and even at a pace which was 'rather terrorising'. At this level he was a fast bowler rather than a fast-medium bowler.

Before the tourists arrived, Falcon turned out for MCC against Yorkshire. Coming on as the fifth bowler he took five for 16, helping to dismiss Yorkshire for 124. The game was not finished, but *The Times* stated that he varied his pace intelligently and bowled with considerably more fire than for the University in 1911.

The tourists duly visited Norfolk and Falcon was selected for both fixtures. The Australians came to Lakenham in late August to play an 'England XI', but the game coincided with the bad weather and

---

13   To this day, this remains the highest number of wickets taken by a Norfolk bowler in a Minor Counties Championship season. Falconer played just seven first-class games, for Northamptonshire between 1907 and 1910, securing nine wickets in all.

proved to be a disappointing, damp squib both as a spectacle as a whole and specifically for the two Norfolk players in the England side. At opposite ends of their respective careers, Falcon and George Raikes, barely troubled the scorers with the bat and Raikes bowled but two fruitless overs before rain terminated the proceedings. Falcon didn't get a bowl at all which must have been desperately disappointing for him. He did, at least, take three catches.

The fixture against the South Africans at Old Buckenham (a village about twelve miles south-west of Norwich) in September, provided Falcon with a much better showcase in which to display his talent as an up-and-coming pace bowler. Lionel Robinson's XI[14] batted first and had struggled to 30 for five when Falcon came in. Although not comfortable with the bowling of Sid Pegler, he defied the attack for 65 minutes, making the second top-score of 29 in an innings total of 153. Given the new ball, he tore into the South African batting, taking four of the first five wickets to fall at a personal cost of only eight runs. Having collapsed to 17 for five, South Africa reached close of play at a precarious 34 for five. Michael Falcon finished with figures of six for 47 the next day. In the second innings he bowled a solitary maiden as the South Africans collapsed against Frank Tarrant and Harry Simms on a treacherous wicket – the former took five wickets for just eight runs – but it could now be said that he had truly arrived on the international scene.

1913

Norfolk continued to impress in the Minor Counties Championship in 1913, reaching the Challenge Match for the third time in four years. Michael Falcon had another successful season with the bat, scoring over 400 runs. Again he scored all round the wicket with 'clean, powerful driving' a feature of his game. Against Bedfordshire, he and Reginald Popham put on 197 for the first wicket in only 100 minutes: he moved from 61 to 155 in a little over half an hour. With the ball he took 36 wickets, including five five-wicket returns. He bowled with 'great pace'. Several batsmen were deceived by his 'swerver'. His captaincy, too, earned plaudits, ex-England skipper Archie MacLaren being favourably impressed.

---

14   Lionel Robinson's role in Norfolk cricket and his involvement with ex-Test skipper Archie MacLaren will be dealt with in Chapter Nine.

The Gentlemen's side which played at Lord's, 14, 15 and 16 July 1913.
Standing (l to r): H.L.Simms, P.G.H.Fender, M.Falcon, E.L.Kidd.
Seated: F.R.Foster, G.L.Jessop, P.F.Warner (capt), J.W.H.T.Douglas,
D.C.Robinson (wk).
On the ground: S.G.Smith, R.B.Lagden.

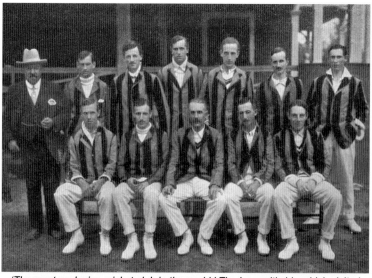

'The most exclusive cricket club in the world.' The Incogniti side which visited
Philadelphia and New York in September 1913.
Standing (l to r): G.Freeman (umpire), C.H.Eiloart, G.R.R.Colman, Hon
H.G.H.Mulholland, D.M.P.Whitcombe (wk), C.L.St J.Tudor, B.G. von B.Melle.
Seated: M.Falcon, P.Collins, E.J.Metcalfe, W.G.M.Sarel, C.E.Hatfeild.

Michael Falcon continued to play social cricket alongside his county commitments. He dominated what was entitled 'Honingham Week',[15] turning out for R.T.Fellowes' XI in three matches in rural Norfolk with Test stars such as Sid Pegler, Bernard Bosanquet and Archie MacLaren amongst his opponents. He missed two of Norfolk's Championship matches: once because he was representing the Gentlemen at Lord's, but, remarkably, he was also absent from the Challenge Match as he was touring the USA with the Incogniti club. This might seem in the light of today's priorities as something of a dereliction of duty by Falcon, but in those more carefree days an opportunity to travel abroad was too good to resist. Indeed it was the only overseas tour he was able to make during his long career, apart from brief trips across the Irish Sea with Cambridge University in 1908 and 1910.

From the published description, the Incog tour was an elaborate affair, starting off with a dinner on 26 August, at the house of the captain, Col Cleveland Greenway, at 27 Ovington Square, Chelsea. The touring party comprised seventeen overall, three ladies (players' wives), a professional umpire and thirteen players, nine of whom had played first-class cricket. The captain was 48, but most of the others were 'young blades', mostly well under 30. They were seen off from Waterloo by a group of eleven, including H.D.G. 'Shrimp' Leveson Gower. They arrived back in Plymouth on 6 October.

The standard of the cricket was high – two of the matches were against Philadelphia representative sides[16] – and the tour was one of the last occasions that North American cricket flickered in the public spotlight before slipping into obscurity. (At one point, Incogniti were accounted by their hosts as 'the most exclusive cricket club in the world' which perhaps hints at the Anglophile mindset of American cricket at the time.) Michael Falcon played in all six fixtures, four of which the Incogniti won, with one drawn and one lost. He had mixed fortunes with the bat, scoring a century against Merion, the leading club in Philadelphia, but failing to reach fifty in any other innings. He was more successful with the ball, being the leading wicket-taker, with 38 victims at an average of 13.11. Falcon's personal highlight of the tour was in the final

---

15   Honingham is a Norfolk village near East Dereham not easy to get to, even in the twenty-first century.

16   Three matches played by Philadelphian sides, against an Australian touring team in June of the same year, are classified as first-class.

game, against Philadelphia C.C., when the Incogniti came up against Bart King in a twelve-a-side contest. It was a case of an up-and-coming paceman in Falcon confronting an old master in King who was one of the very first bowlers to master the art of swing bowling. Writing in the 1920s, 'Plum' Warner rated King as 'at least the equal of the greatest of them all'. Australian Test player Herbert Hordern, a team-mate of King in Philadelphia and an opponent of Sydney Barnes in an Ashes series, rated Barnes slightly the better bowler, but it is clear that King was a very great player who would have played many Tests had he been born in England or Australia. In common with Falcon, he was approached by at least one English county with a view to qualifying to play in the County Championship.

The Incogniti batted first and King ran through the later batting to take seven for 46 as the tourists were shot out for 139. Fighting back, the Incogniti bowled Philadelphia out for 128, Falcon taking four for 58. The tourists again failed to shine in the second innings, making 129; King's five wickets cost 49 runs. Set 141 to win, Philadelphia were routed by Falcon, who took eight for 14, and made only 61. In his published account of the tour, Falcon says, in this match, that he 'made the ball jump' and 'turn in from the off', adding that his figures 'tell their own story'.

The report of the tour makes it plain that it was a highly sociable affair. There are references to 'bachelors who were a hit with members of the fairer sex'; Freeman having 'a bit of a head' one morning; sightseeing at Niagara; dinners and dances, including learning the then new-fangled 'tango'; going to a big baseball game; and various golf, tennis and bridge parties. Geoffrey Colman and Falcon, Norfolk 'co-optees' on the tour, won many of the sporting competitions the players had between themselves. When asked of his impression of America by his son many years later, Falcon remembered the hosts as being overly fond of their cocktails, which they consumed at any excuse. (Falcon was himself a moderate drinker.)

He enjoyed his trip, but whether he would have gone if he had known that he would never lead his beloved Norfolk to the Minor Counties Championship is a moot point. At this period Norfolk were a very strong team and Falcon must have felt sure that more titles would come his way in the passage of time. Although they came close on several occasions between the Wars, they always fell short for one reason or another.

In his absence, Norfolk struggled through the Challenge Match against Glamorgan, winning on the first-innings in a rain-affected match. Thanks to an innings of 74 by Reginald Popham, Norfolk accumulated a total of 244 and Glamorgan were limited to a mere 168 by the bowling of Roderick Falconer and Eric Fulcher, both of who took five wickets. In the little time remaining Norfolk collapsed ignominiously to the bowling of Harry Creber (eight for 33) and were dismissed for a humiliating 61 runs. The award of the Championship to Norfolk, on the strength of their first-innings lead, was thus somewhat tarnished. This unsatisfactory situation led the Minor Counties Association to alter its rules so that a first-innings lead did not constitute a result in such games: under the new ruling an outright win would be required. Norfolk and Glamorgan had both finished with a percentage of 72.50; as joint table-toppers they would presumably have shared the title under the new ruling.

In the first-class arena, Falcon took five for 55 for Lionel Robinson's XI against Cambridge University and then starred for the Gentlemen at The Oval. Batting at number eleven – a ludicrous position given his record to date – he helped Gilbert Jessop add 58 for the last wicket after the Gentlemen had collapsed to 81 for nine. Then he took six for 58, with the last five wickets falling in 20 balls, to help dismiss the Players for 131, thereby allowing his side to achieve a draw. The *Daily Telegraph* described his bowling as 'magnificent' and 'superb' and praised his attractive action.

The ball with which Falcon took six for 58 in the Players' first innings at The Oval in 1913.

1914

Norfolk had high hopes as the 1914 season started, but results were not as good as in the previous two years and only two of the first seven games were won. However, the side remained unbeaten until Falcon was called away, being 'engaged in national service', and forced to miss the last game of the season against Cambridgeshire. In his absence, Norfolk went down to defeat. Even before this, the declaration of war on Germany (on 4 August) had affected the season, causing the abandonment of the home fixture with Staffordshire, who pleaded that the dislocation of the rail network caused by mobilisation made it more than inconvenient for them to travel to Lakenham.

Michael Falcon had yet another consistent season with the bat, amassing over 300 runs in seven matches, with a top score of 93 against Hertfordshire. This innings took but 98 minutes and was, like most of his aggressive innings, characterised by drives of splendid power on both sides of the wicket. At other times circumstances dictated caution and he was also praised for his defence. He was the spearhead of the bowling attack, taking 39 wickets at under 15 apiece. Two six-wicket hauls against Cambridgeshire were the highlight as he made the ball swerve a good deal and come through at a nasty height on a pitch which gave him some assistance. Earlier in the year, at Bedford, spectators were treated to a forerunner of a 'Carmody' field when Falcon deployed no fewer than five slips.

In retrospect, Falcon would have viewed his performance for the Free Foresters against Cambridge University with mixed emotions. He took 13 wickets in the match, comfortably his best performance in first-class cricket, but paradoxically played a highly significant part in his side's defeat. Having been rested, he was brought back into the attack, with his figures standing at an impressive seven for 54, when the University needed 16 runs to win and had its last pair at the crease. He found himself bowling to Geoffrey Davies – himself the taker of eleven wickets in the match – who promptly hit him for four fours in five balls to win the match.

The Free Foresters, 1912-1936

Although Michael Falcon's choice to play for Norfolk meant his appearances in first-class cricket were sporadic, there was one first-class club to which he offered considerable loyalty – this was the Free Foresters. More specifically, he participated in and eventually helped to organise the annual match between the Free Foresters and Cambridge University. The Free Foresters were one of the most senior of the wandering clubs founded in the Victorian era, arising in 1856 when an eleven raised by the three brothers Armistead travelled to Sutton Coldfield to play against the team of

Rev W.K.R.Bedford on its new ground. In 1866 it was formalised that 'the design of the Free Foresters is to play matches with County, Varsity, College and Regimental XIs and with recognised clubs in desirable localities'.

To anyone leafing through the pages of *The Cricketer* between the wars, it can be seen that the Free Foresters were a thriving club who actively fulfilled their mission, playing many matches, against a wide range of opponents. Certain names crop up repeatedly on the team sheet, but membership was large and many players would only play one or two matches a season. Household names such as Douglas Jardine, Errol Holmes and Freddie Brown all made appearances when they could spare the time. For the annual game at Fenner's the Free Foresters' team would contain a predominance of old Light Blues: in 1927 and 1931 ten of the team were old Blues whilst in 1933 the entire team had represented Cambridge against Oxford.

Where the Free Foresters differed from the other wandering clubs was in their status when they played Oxford and Cambridge Universities. From 1912 onward,[17] these matches were awarded first-class status and assumed an important place in the Oxbridge season. Michael Falcon was involved at the earliest possible opportunity, turning out to play against Cambridge at Fenner's on 10 June 1912. The University scored 250 and in reply the Free Foresters collapsed for 107. Seizing his chance with the new ball, Falcon then took six for 37 as he and William Greswell, bowling unchanged, shot out the students for 74. The Free Foresters' early batting failed again, with the exception of Norman Druce, who made an unbeaten 152 out of 218 for five and carried his side to what turned out to be a comfortable victory.

Michael Falcon did not play in the Cambridge fixtures of 1913, 1919, 1921 or 1924, but after this intermittent start he became an ever-present in the Free Foresters against the Light Blues until he made his final appearance in 1936, his last first-class game, at the age of 47.[18] He did not turn out in many matches against teams other than Cambridge University, preferring to play most of his social cricket in Norfolk. He did, however appear against Oxford

---

17   The club played first-class matches against Cambridge until 1962 and against Oxford until 1968.

18   Falcon's final first-class game was a damp anticlimax as rain prevented any play on the first day and a dull draw was inevitable.

University in 1920, 1921 and 1931 and in a few other non first-class fixtures.

When Falcon started playing for the Free Foresters, he was at the height of his powers; as late as 1926 he opened both the batting and the bowling. However by 1936 he was well past his best. Although he was still able to hold his own playing for Norfolk in the Minor Counties Championship, first-class cricket was a different matter. In his last first-class match, aged 47, he batted at eleven and bowled only three overs.[19] Even so, he sold his wicket dearly, and remained not out in five of his last six first-class innings. His last day of note with the ball was in 1931 when he took four for 54 against Oxford University. The inevitable falling-off in his performances with age affected Michael Falcon's returns for the Free Foresters, but his career figures in 20 first-class matches for the wandering club were highly creditable: 692 runs at 27.68 and 71 wickets at 26.46. Perhaps more than any other first-class cricketer, games for the Free Foresters played a significant part in Falcon's first-class career. With the ball, no fewer than seven of his 20 first-class five-wicket hauls were taken for the wandering club: the highlight being his rout, referred to earlier, of the Cambridge University batsmen in 1914 when he took six for 41 and seven for 70. This was the only time he took ten wickets in a first-class match, and his second innings return was also a career best. With the bat, Falcon made three fifties, with 77 not out against Oxford University (in 1921) and 77 and an unbeaten 86 against Cambridge University (in 1925 and 1926 respectively), the highlights of his returns.

MCC Committee man, 1914-1938

On 13 May 1914, the brilliant amateur batsman Reginald Foster died of diabetes at the early age of 36. This left a place vacant on the MCC Committee and Michael Falcon was co-opted to fill the gap. He was only 25 at the time and it was both a great honour and a mark of the esteem in which he was held at Lord's that he should be asked to serve at such a young age, working alongside many of the great names in cricket history. To emphasize his relative youth

---

19   A generation later another ex-Cambridge all-rounder made it a habit to turn out for the Free Foresters against the University. 'Gubby' Allen played until he was over fifty but, unlike Falcon, he retained the ability to perform at the first-class level as a relatively old man; in the seven years he played he scored no fewer than four centuries and averaged 84.50 with the bat.

it can be noted that the next youngest member of the committee was Jack Mason, then fourteen years older than Falcon, whilst the other younger members were 'Plum' Warner and 'Shrimp' Leveson Gower, both a year older than Mason. To add to the contrast, Mason, Warner and Leveson Gower all had experience both of Test cricket and of the regular first-class county game, whilst Falcon's experience was limited to the University seasons, a few friendlies and the Minor Counties Championship.

As it turned out, Falcon was only able to attend a couple of committee meetings before he was called away to serve in the First World War, but once that conflict was over he had an opportunity to return to it. Proposed by Stanley Christopherson and seconded by William Patterson, he was duly elected in 1919 and continued to serve until 1938. The constitution of the General Committee meant that he had to 'retire by rotation' every few years and seek re-election. In this he was invariably successful, but it was not quite a formality as evidenced by the 1929 election in which Falcon and Viscount Ullswater received an equal number of votes and he had to be specially chosen to continue to serve. That there was an element of a 'closed shop' about the committee has to be admitted: Falcon and his close friend Frank Mann advanced each other's candidacy during the 1920s.

In June 1919, Michael Falcon was appointed a member of the Cricket and Selection sub-Committee, where he was joined by such famous figures as Lord Harris, Lord Hawke and 'Plum' Warner. On this sub-committee he had a part in the selection of the 1920/21 Ashes touring side. Having proved to have a safe pair of hands, he was given the chairmanship of his own sub-committee in 1924. Whilst directing the Tennis and Racquets sub-Committee may not have been the most glamorous of tasks, Falcon served with diligence throughout the mid- and late-twenties and was returned to the more prestigious Cricket and Selection sub-Committee in 1929.

In 1933 the MCC Committee was involved in the famous exchange of telegrams with the Australian Cricket Board of Control regarding what came to be known as 'bodyline' bowling. Michael Falcon had sent a letter regretting his inability to attend the relevant meeting and so was not involved in the early stages of the discussions regarding 'bodyline'. He was, however, appointed to the special sub-committee whose task was to debate the question of 'leg-theory as practised by fast bowlers'. Also on the sub-committee, which delivered its report on 29 October 1934, were Lord Hawke, Sir Stanley Jackson and 'Plum' Warner. The sub-committee is noteworthy for the limited experience of its members in the art of bowling. Only Sir Stanley Jackson and Michael Falcon had any notable records as bowlers, and 'Jacker' was only fast-medium in pace; Falcon alone on the sub-committee knew what it was like to render an opposing batsman unconscious. The minutes of MCC committee meetings are notoriously uninformative, so one can but speculate as to what influence Falcon would have exerted as the 'in-house' expert when set alongside the powerful influences of the senior figures on the sub-committee. In aiding their deliberations one assumes that the sub-committee would have had the reports on the tour of the skipper Douglas Jardine and the two managers, 'Plum' Warner and Richard Palairet; in addition these three, plus Harold Larwood, Bill Voce and Les Ames were called to Lord's for interview.[20] David Frith, the author of *Bodyline Autopsy*, the most thorough investigation into the whole affair, noted that none of the relevant paperwork survives. That the sub-committee eventually ruled 'bodyline' to be undesirable is well-known and further comment is unnecessary here.

Falcon returned to the stewardship of the Tennis and Rackets sub-Committee in 1935, which occupied him until his involvement with the MCC Committee ceased in 1938. Until the last couple of years his record of attendance at Committee meetings had been good: the decline in the frequency of his attendance may have been due to the difficulty in reaching London whilst raising a young family in the rural backwater of North Burlingham. Whatever may be the case, Falcon's efforts behind the scenes at Lord's echo his work on committees in Norfolk and attest to his love for cricket and his desire to work on its behalf.[21]

---

20   Warner would have probably wanted the support of 'Gubby' Allen, who had refused to bowl bodyline, but he seems to have been on very bad terms with the MCC secretary, Billy Findlay, at the relevant time. Allen was able to exert his influence later whilst attending meetings of the Advisory County Cricket Committee, a forum for the skippers of first-class counties, in which he spoke openly against 'bodyline'.

21   As a player he had appeared in eight first-class fixtures for the premier club between 1911 and 1929, and, closer to the grass roots, in one or two lesser 'out-matches' a year in most seasons until 1931.

The Falcon brothers at War, 1914-1918

During the First World War all three Falcon brothers served at a variety of fronts. Michael senior and Isabella must have feared for the safety of their sons but, unlike so many families on both sides, the Falcons were lucky and the three brothers survived the War without so much as a scratch between them.[22] Little evidence remains today of the service records of the Falcons, the archives having sustained heavy damage during the Second World War, but a summary of what is known will give a taste of what they underwent.

Michael Falcon in the Royal Field Artillery, in Palestine in 1918.

---

22   Norfolk cricket as a whole was not as fortunate as the Falcon family during the Great War. No fewer than six players, all of them officers, were killed in action: Gervase Birkbeck, George Carter, Vincent Hoare, Sydney Page, Eric Penn and Ralph Thurgar, M.C. After the war a memorial was erected in the pavilion at Lakenham; it was unveiled by the Norfolk chairman Ernest Raikes and dedicated by Rev H.B.J.Armstrong, in the presence of Michael Falcon and Henry Grierson, the captain of Bedfordshire, against whom Norfolk were then playing.

Michael Falcon served in the Royal Field Artillery, in an East Anglian Brigade; he reached the rank of captain and, according to the Royal Norfolk Regimental Museum, served in Gallipoli and Palestine. The Museum suggests that he was involved with the Norfolk yeomanry, adding that the yeomanry were often associated with the artillery. The *Who's Who of British Members of Parliament* and the *Eastern Daily Press* also link him to the Territorials and credit him with serving in France as well as the Middle East. He was mentioned in despatches by Lord Allenby whilst serving in Palestine in 1918; he was still stationed there when the call came from England for him to stand as a candidate in the 1918 election.

Harry Falcon also served in the Royal Field Artillery, being linked both to the 1st East Anglian and the 266th Brigades. He served on the western front and attained the rank of major. William Falcon joined the Royal Engineers and was also attached to the Transport Corps. Like his older brother Michael, he served in Gallipoli and Palestine, where he was also mentioned in despatches, and also reached the rank of captain; he was an acting major when the War finished.

Chapter Four
At Westminster

When a general election was called at the end of the Great War, the Liberals and the Conservatives (still widely known at that time as the Unionists) decided to field a combined slate of candidates and, hopefully, form another coalition government. In the previous six elections, stretching over a period of 26 years, the seat of East Norfolk had returned a Liberal, Sir Robert Price. Learning that he would not be returned unopposed, he decided to stand down, citing his age, 65, as the reason. At this point there was no official candidate in place and the scene was set for some political sharp practice.

The 'Khaki' election, 1918

The Conservatives moved much faster than the Liberals, and John Cator, the chairman of the East Norfolk Unionist Association, announced the adoption of Captain Michael Falcon as the Unionist Coalition candidate for the constituency on 9 November. Falcon was duly cabled in Palestine, where he was serving, sent back his assent, and, like many other soldier candidates, was summoned home. (The presence of so many candidates from the armed services led to this election being known as the 'Khaki' election.) As luck would have it there was a Yarmouth drifter docked in Haifa, close to where Falcon was stationed, manned by a crew from Winterton. This enabled the prospective coalition candidate to reach home quickly. Quite why Captain Falcon was chosen by the Unionists to contest East Norfolk remains unclear. He had never expressed interest in a political career before the War, his sole deed of a political nature being to support 'Plum' Warner in speaking in favour of conscription at a public meeting in King's Lynn.[23] Perhaps the local Unionists thought that, as a well-known

---

23   At Cambridge, for instance, there is no record of Falcon joining the Union Society, which would have been the first port of call for any undergraduate with an interest in a political career.

local sportsman, he could attract a sizeable 'personal' vote which might prove crucial if the contest were to be close.

The Liberals, having been pre-empted, complained bitterly and put forward their own candidate, also under the coalition banner, to oppose the Unionist. Mr Fred Henderson was chosen: he grizzled about the adoption of Falcon but attached no blame to the Unionist personally as he had been in Palestine at the time when Cator had jumped the gun. To complete the field, Mr William Taylor was nominated by the National Farmers' Union (NFU) under the 'Agriculture and Labour' banner. It was expected that he would pick up the majority of the Labour vote.

Captain Falcon received a letter, a confirmation which became known as a 'coupon', from Lloyd George and Bonar Law (respectively leaders of the Liberal and Unionist parties in Parliament) endorsing him as the official coalition candidate ahead of Mr Henderson. He returned to Norfolk and turned his attention to canvassing. He found himself thrust into the deep end immediately, being scheduled to speak at Wroxham Village Hall virtually straight off the boat. To his consternation he was asked a long and convoluted question about housing, a subject about which he knew virtually nothing. According to his son Michael Gascoigne, his rather lame and abject response was to say, 'We can't all live in castles' and hope for the best. Much to his amazement his answer provoked widespread cheers and applause. Turning to the Unionist party activist sitting next to him at the speakers' table, he furtively asked what on earth was going on, only to be told that the man who had asked the question was the owner of the local public house which, by happy fortune, was called 'The Castle Inn'. His campaign was thus up and running to a good start.

At a meeting at Blofield, Falcon apologized that his military duties had left him out of touch, but he thought that the men who had been abroad should have some representatives in Parliament. He was anxious to stand as a Coalition candidate in order to support Mr Lloyd George in making a good peace: the one man the soldiers had always known to be at their backs was Lloyd George. He then elaborated on the Coalition programme at some length.

All three candidates appeared on the same platform at North Walsham, addressing a female audience. Falcon stated that he always had at heart the health of the people and one of the main ways of ensuring it was to have good and healthy homes. It was fortunate that women were having the vote now when these things were being considered. Women were the home-makers and they were the people who knew what things ought to be like. He added that he was in favour of immediate housing reform.

Despite large attendances at the various meetings, there was apathy on polling day itself, 14 December, and fewer voters were seen in East Norfolk than in neighbouring constituencies. Captain Falcon set out early on a motor tour of as much of the division as time permitted. The count, which was conducted in the Norwich Shirehall, did not take place until 28 December, with Gerald Blake – once Norfolk's wicket-keeper – officiating as acting deputy returning officer. The results were as follows:

Captain M.Falcon (Coalition Unionist)	7,030
F.Henderson (Independent Coalition)	6,691
W.B.Taylor (Agriculture and Labour)	1,926
Majority	339

Thus Captain Falcon was narrowly elected to serve as MP for Norfolk East. He thanked the returning officer and declared that it was a most pleasant and friendly contest. This feeling was echoed by the other two candidates: there was no evidence of any hard feelings from Mr Henderson on being pre-empted as the official Coalition candidate.

Michael Falcon practised as a barrister from these chambers at 3 Essex Court, Temple in the twenties.

For the first part of his political career, Captain Falcon combined his Parliamentary duties with work at the bar, where he had chambers at 3 Essex Court in the Temple. In the House, Falcon's attention was largely taken up by rural problems, which continued to occupy him for the whole of his time as an MP. When the prime minister, Bonar Law, announced that the government was to appoint a Commission to look into agriculture, Falcon and numerous other interested parties in Norfolk readied themselves to give evidence to the new body.

The NFU were also active and Falcon replied to a letter from their Norfolk branch which had asked for his support. Although he was broadly sympathetic to their views, he stated that to get agreement between farmers and farm labourers would not be easy, and that he must represent the labourers as well as their employers. The NFU were not entirely impressed by his reply, but he did at least proffer one which was more than can be said of his fellow Norfolk MPs. The hostility of the farmers was a recurring theme in Falcon's political career.

In November 1919, Captain Falcon spoke at North Walsham, saying that Norfolk faced a serious set of problems but that he remained optimistic. He stressed, not for the only time, the need for the country to grow as much food as possible and hoped that farm labourers would receive their due rewards. He was then asked, again not for the only time, why, when he had claimed to be against conscription early in the year, he had voted for it in the recent Army Bill. He explained that he had changed his mind because of the need to station troops in India and Egypt and the need to keep a sizeable force on the Continent to keep Germany in line. He stated that the need for troops should drop until May 1920, by when there should be an army of 500,000, all of them volunteers.

Not long after this meeting, Falcon spoke at Old Catton and Drayton, making his usual plea for a fair balance between the farmers and their labourers. He lamented the increase in the National Debt, saying that there was a need for increased industrial production and hoping that strike action would be reduced by recent legislation; he did, however, concede that the working man had a right to withhold his labour if he so wished.

Defending his decision to vote against the coalition government in August 1920, Falcon said that he disapproved of the way it was spending money. Again he conceded the value of trade unions but cautioned strongly against the dangers of socialism.

In the House of Commons, Falcon asked the Attorney General if he was aware that, due to increases in the cost of living and in taxation, judges were finding it difficult to carry out social duties required by their position. The Attorney General agreed, saying that the matter was of great importance and would be dealt with shortly. Falcon also spoke on the predicament of many ex-officers and men who would soon finish their training in agriculture in accordance with the training scheme and who would be eligible for smallholdings. Norfolk County Council had a dearth of land available for distribution, so that the ex-soldiers were being thrown back on their savings, with the result that, when they did receive their land, they had no capital with which to set up their businesses. Replying for the government, Sir Robert Sanders stonewalled somewhat but said that the Council would be urged to expedite the provision of smallholdings.

Captain Falcon criticised the government again when it dropped the Agriculture Bill in September 1921 stating that, as a purely agricultural constituency, East Norfolk would have benefited greatly from the adoption of the Bill.

At the end of 1921 Falcon found himself returning to the scene of his childhood on official business. He was awarded the honour of unveiling the war memorial at Horstead, following which he addressed the crowd and a bugler played *The Last Post* and *Reveille*. His younger brother, Major Harry Falcon, was in command of the party of over forty ex-servicemen who were present at the ceremony.

A second election, 1922

The coalition government of Liberals and Conservatives did not survive the duration of the 1918 parliament and, in 1922, the two parties stood in opposition to each other as well as the Labour Party. Activity to unseat Captain Falcon started early, with the NFU selecting Mr James Wright to run as an agricultural candidate and the Liberals adopting Mr Hugh Seely, who declared himself to be a plain, straightforward Liberal and a believer in free trade.

Captain Falcon was busy in Parliament in the first half of 1922, being involved in a plethora of issues, but with the problems of agriculture taking up much of his time as usual. In his absence from his constituency, he was defended by party workers against criticism from the NFU, and Sir John Green stated that, as the honorary secretary of the Agricultural Commission of the House of Commons, he could testify to all the good work being done in the field of agriculture by Falcon.

Returning to speak in Norfolk, Captain Falcon said that the political crisis had been going on for some years and would continue regardless of the date of the next election. Personally, he had supported the coalition government, as he had been elected to do, even though it had sometimes made mistakes but its time was over. He dismissed Mr Seely's manifesto as 'specious' and, whilst describing Mr Wright as an honourable man, he said that an MP should support all his constituents, not just a minority (*i.e.* the farmers). From this and other comments, perhaps we should think of him as a 'one-nation' Tory, in the Disraeli tradition.

At a meeting of the Eastern Provincial Division of the National Unionist Association, Captain Falcon seconded a plea that the government should reduce taxation in order to revive trade and promote employment. He called, in particular, for reductions in the duty on tea and beer, and in income tax.

There was a pleasant surprise at the annual meeting of the East Norfolk Conservative Association in that a member of the NFU, Mr Werner Cook, broke ranks and said that he was doing his best to get Captain Falcon re-elected as he was true to his word in trying to do his best for all his constituents. In a response to criticism from the NFU party line, Captain Falcon declared he was as opposed to the 'old-time crusty Toryism of the past' as he was to the leftist extremists. He stated that the two great industries of East Anglia were agriculture and fishing and that he would do his utmost to encourage both: a theme he would return again and again during his campaign. Soon after this speech it was announced that he was giving up his legal practice in order to concentrate on his parliamentary duties.

There was then a major surprise in the campaigning when Mr Wright withdrew his candidacy, to be replaced by a Labour candidate, Mr George Hewitt. Mr Wright said he was withdrawing in order to avoid taking votes from Captain Falcon, whom he would now prefer to be elected. At this point Falcon had not yet been formally adopted as the Conservative candidate, but the formalities were soon dealt with. At a meeting of the East Norfolk Conservatives, chairman John Cator stated that the constituency were fortunate in having Captain Falcon as their MP. He was, at the last election, 'a Unionist holding Conservative views ... he remained a Conservative and he would fight as a Conservative. He had had his problems with agriculture, having had to refuse to adopt the programme of the NFU because he had to represent the interests of all his constituents. He would co-operate with the Liberals against Labour.' Captain Falcon was unanimously elected candidate and expressed his determination to win the seat. In his campaign he was greatly aided by Mr Reginald Neville and Sir John Green.[24]

Captain Falcon campaigned on his work for the constituency since 1918. For example, he had obtained a government grant of £3,000 for the Fleggs[25] in relief of unemployment and, in Blofield, when the Ministry of Health refused permission for the local authority to proceed with its housing scheme, he had lobbied hard and managed to secure approval for at least half the plan.

He continued to campaign hard on the issues of agriculture and fishing, stating that farm labourers were especially deserving of government support but warning that it would be unwise to raise labourers' wages before agriculture was restored to a sound enough footing. Referring to a recent conference held in Norwich between landowners, farmers and labourers with the object of restoring prosperity to agriculture, Falcon stated that, if re-elected, he would support the proposals arising from this meeting to help get farming back on its feet.

At this point in the hustings, Captain Falcon was the subject of some hard criticism, in the form of a letter to the *Eastern Daily Press* written by the Liberal candidate, Mr Seely, who attacked his attendance record in the House of Commons. He defended his absences from the House, saying that he was always 'paired', a response which didn't entirely placate Mr Seely. Speaking of the accusation made by the Liberals that he voted to repeal the Agriculture Act, he denied the claim point-blank, saying that 'I was in Norfolk attending to my constituency – not playing cricket – and I paired with another member who was in favour of repealing the Act.' By referring to his cricketing activities explicitly, Captain Falcon was acknowledging that balancing his parliamentary duties with his role as Norfolk skipper was a genuine issue. In 1922 he played 14 times for Norfolk and was also involved in one first-class game. However this was the only time in either the 1922 or 1923 election campaigns in which his potential conflict of interests was raised. Despite Mr Seely's letter the *Eastern Daily Press* was moved to say that the contest in East Norfolk 'was marked by the utmost good humour on all sides and might be described as a model

---

24   Falcon's voting record had shown himself to be of an independent mind: when he did not agree with the official Coalition policy he voted against it. If the Coalition had remained in being this free-thinking might have attracted strong criticism, but the Unionists had no qualms about re-adopting him as their own candidate.

25   The Fleggs are the area to the north of Great Yarmouth.

election. Principles were put before everything else, and the candidates ... were given fair hearings and, although pointed questions were frequently put to them, questioners, if not satisfied with the answers returned, did not openly show their disappointment.'

On 15 November, the day of polling, Captain Falcon was as energetic as in the 1918 election, visiting 32 polling stations in the large rural constituency. Counting took place in the Norwich Shirehall on the following day and the figures were formally announced by the High Sheriff, Mr E.G.Buxton. The result was declared shortly before 4.00pm and was as follows:

Captain M.Falcon (Conservative)	9,270
H.M.Seely (Liberal)	8,962
G.Hewitt (Labour)	4,361
Majority	308

Thus Captain Falcon was narrowly re-elected MP for East Norfolk. It was agreed by all the candidates that the contest was very fairly conducted, that they were all given a fair hearing and that principles were put before anything else.

Falcon Unseated, 1923

In March 1923, Captain Falcon visited the Town Hall at Loddon for a meeting chaired by Mr C.R.Cadge, who, referring to a letter written to the *Eastern Daily Press* which expressed the opinion that Falcon did not speak often enough in the House of Commons, and claimed that the MP had had no luck 'catching the speaker's eye' on numerous occasions. In truth, the bear pit that was the floor of the House was not a natural hunting ground for a man described in Lemmon and Smith's *Votes For Cricket* as 'quiet and modest'. Although Captain Falcon had made numerous speeches in 1919, mostly concerned with the provision of training for ex-soldiers and the problems of agriculture, his appearances in *Hansard* dropped away sharply in the following years. That he was all too aware of this is evidenced by his commencing a speech in 1922 with the words, 'As one who seldom intervenes in debate ... '. *Hansard* shows that in his five years as an MP he spoke on just twenty-two occasions in the chamber.

The East Norfolk Conservative Association opened its annual meeting in May 1923 with an expression of appreciation of Captain

Falcon's efforts in the House of Commons to improve the condition of agriculture in his constituency. Captain Falcon received a loud ovation, thanked all present for their good work on his behalf and said that he believed agriculture had turned the corner. He was very much encouraged in his work in the House and on the Agricultural Commission by the numerous letters he had received congratulating him on what he had done.

Later in the year Captain Falcon spoke of the difficulties that the current government had to face. Again agriculture was to the fore as he assured all that, as Chairman of the Agricultural Commission,[26] he would do his best to protect all interested parties in the industry, specifically noting that the farm labourers must be adequately rewarded for their toils.

It was at this point that Captain Falcon's political fortune took a distinct downturn. Addressing a meeting at Brooke, he declared himself to be a Conservative free trader by upbringing and conviction but wanted to reserve judgement on the Prime Minister's proposals on trade until they were fully spelt out. He said the government had achieved great things in the past year and he was a supporter of the Safeguarding of Industries Act for professions such as dyeing and barley growing – indeed he had been personally involved in the inquiry into the imposition of a tax on foreign barley – thereby compromising his credentials as a free trader. The problem was that free trade was actually the policy of the Liberal Party, including Captain Falcon's chief opponent, Hugh Seely, whilst the official Conservative Party policy was one of tariffs to protect important industries from malign foreign influences. Having put his foot in it, Falcon spent the rest of the election campaign backtracking, to his obvious discomfort.[27]

---

26 As with the documentation of so much of Falcon's early life, the Parliamentary Archives have almost nothing surviving on the Commission of Agriculture of the relevant period and the name of Falcon does not feature in what little there is left. It does seem unlikely, at first sight, that an MP who seldom spoke in the House, whose attendance record had been questioned and who had demonstrated that he was of an independent mind by voting against the Government when he disagreed with official policy would be entrusted with the care of such an important Commission. However, the only source we have are the long-range reports in the Norfolk press which seem quite convinced that Falcon was playing a major role at Westminster in the field of agricultural policy.

27 To be fair to Falcon, free trade was traditionally the policy of the Conservative Party. Its leader Stanley Baldwin, influenced by grandees such as Stanley Jackson, had done an about-turn on tariff reform for this election. This might have caught Falcon by surprise and left him wrong-footed. (These days, of course, a politician not 'on message' gets a sharp reminder in the form of a mobile phone call from head office.)

Introducing Captain Falcon at a meeting at Acle, John Cator said the MP had the honour of being the chairman of the parliamentary committee appointed to look into the matter of imported malting barley. This sort of post was usually given to a senior MP, so this was a feather in the cap of Falcon and his constituency. Speaking in reply, Captain Falcon said the government had passed some worthwhile legislation in the past year, such as the Housing Act (intended to help with the construction of much-needed housing) and the Workmen's Compensation Act. Measures to help agriculture had also been taken. Falcon claimed it was not a free trade versus protection election but an employment versus unemployment election and that he 'did not tremble at the artillery which he had to face'.

Captain Falcon had to speak in favour of tariffs again a few days later, saying that the unsettled conditions in Europe made them necessary. On the same day, 30 November, he had a letter published in the *Eastern Daily Press* in which he stated that the habit of the Liberal press of calling him a 'Conservative Free Trader' was misleading and that he was a loyal supporter of the Prime Minister. Only a couple of days later he had to explain himself again, saying that under normal conditions he was in favour of free trade but that, in the current post-war chaos, the protection of vulnerable industries was necessary.

The election turned into a re-run of the 1922 campaign with Seely representing the Liberals again and George Hewitt bearing the Labour colours. In his last few addresses Captain Falcon tried to turn the minds of the voters away from the subject of free trade. He stated that the crucial point of the election was the issue of unemployment and he campaigned in favour of an increase in state pensions and of an increase in the wage of farm labourers to 30 shillings a week. The *Norfolk News* commented favourably on Falcon's candidature: 'For the rest Captain Falcon is popular with all classes. A sportsman and a famous cricketer, he has made rapid progress in his political career, and unites with a strong love of Norfolk, and particularly his own division, an attractive personality which in the judgement of his own party, will again place him at the head of the poll.'

On election day, 6 December, the mood was quiet; the *Eastern Daily Press* commenting on the campaign that there was 'the best of feeling displayed on all hands, the candidates were able to place their views before the electors without hindrance or interruption.'

Unfortunately for Captain Falcon, the *Norfolk News* had viewed his prospects through rose-tinted spectacles. On the day there was a considerable swing to the Liberals, the votes being cast as follows:

H.M.Seely (Liberal)	11,807
Captain M.Falcon (Conservative)	8,472
G.Hewitt (Labour)	3,530
Majority	3,335

After the result announcement, Mr Seely proposed a vote of thanks to the returning officer; Captain Falcon, in seconding, congratulated his opponent. Later he said that 'naturally he was disappointed at the result, but he had lived long enough and knocked about the world sufficiently to know that life was full of ups and downs. Captain Falcon asked the press to say that he regrets that his efforts on behalf of the Conservative Party in East Norfolk have not met with success on this occasion. He, however, is most grateful for all the support offered to him and tenders his thanks to all those who cast their votes in his favour at the poll.'

There was a strong swing against the Conservatives across the whole of rural Norfolk. In 1922 the county returned four Conservative MPs, three Liberals and one Labour; but in 1923 only one Conservative was elected, along with three Liberal and four Labour members. To what extent Captain Falcon's setback was due to his particular problems over free trade and tariffs rather than part of a wider political trend is unclear. The defeat did, however, more or less bring Falcon's political career to an end. He was, perhaps, too much of a gentleman for the cut-and-thrust of politics. His campaigns were so well-mannered that the *Eastern Daily Press* commented favourably in both 1922 and 1923; in the House of Commons itself, he had trouble asserting himself. However he had taken and held what was a Liberal stronghold and also acquitted himself reasonably well in his duties behind the scenes at Westminster. As a member for a rural constituency he was constantly having to jockey for position, trapped between the aspirations of farmers and the demands of farm labourers.

Why Falcon chose to quit politics at this point will remain forever unclear – perhaps he realised he just wasn't ruthless enough to make an effective Member of Parliament. Careful reading of Lemmon and Smith's *Votes For Cricket* reveals that, whilst there have been many members of the House of Lords who have played high-quality cricket whilst sitting in Parliament (albeit mostly in

Victorian times), almost no members of the House of Commons have practised politics and played high-quality cricket at the same time. In the twentieth century there were only four cricketers who played in first-class matches while in membership of the House of Commons.[28] There have been none this century.

Marriage

On 22 June 1920, the engagement was announced of Captain Michael Falcon, MP, eldest son of Mr and Mrs Michael Falcon of Horstead House, Norwich and Kathleen, only daughter of Captain and Mrs Clifton Gascoigne, of Southbroom House, Devizes. Falcon and his father-in-law to-be had known each other for years; Captain Gascoigne, who was from a military family, was quite active on the Norfolk social cricket circle in Edwardian times and was a player of some talent: he appeared twice for Norfolk in 1908, keeping wicket, against Bedfordshire and the Free Foresters, playing alongside his future son-in-law in the latter match.[29] He had been for many years secretary of the Norfolk Territorial Forces Association.

The marriage subsequently took place on 21 September of the same year – after the cricket season had ended, naturally. The ceremony took place on a Tuesday afternoon at the Church of St. Paul's, Knightsbridge. In the *Norfolk News,* there was a brief summary of Falcon's political and cricketing careers which need no repeating here, with the exception of the titbit that, whilst playing 'last season' for the Free Foresters, he had bowled the captain of the Cambridge University eleven with a delivery which sent one of the bails as far as 51 yards, 2 feet from the wicket: not near the record but still impressive for a 31-year-old fast bowler. Turning to the bride, the *Norfolk News* stated that, although she was currently resident in Wiltshire, she had lived most of her life in Norfolk.

---

28   Falcon played 17 matches while representing East Norfolk. The other three were Lord Dalmeny, who played 58 matches, mostly as Surrey's captain, between 1906 and 1908, while representing Edinburgh as a Liberal; Peter Eckersley, a former Lancashire captain, who played a couple of matches, for MCC in 1936 and for an England XI in 1938, while Conservative member for Manchester Exchange; and Aidan Crawley, who played four matches for Kent, MCC and Free Foresters between 1947 and 1949, when he was Labour MP for Buckingham.

29   In 1912, he played for MCC against Norfolk, when he was bowled by Falcon.

That the wedding was a significant one on the social scene was indicated by the status of the officiating clergy: the Rev Hon Edward Lyttelton D.D., an ex-headmaster of Eton College, and the Rev Cyril Alington D.D., his successor at Eton, were the celebrants.[30] After the ceremony there was a reception, not far from the church, at 36 Wilton Crescent; a venue kindly lent to the Gascoignes by Mr and Mrs George Tebbitt. The presents were displayed and included a set of silver candlesticks and fruit dishes from Norfolk C.C.C. and a barometer inscribed 'Presented by the tradesmen of Horstead, Coltishall and District'.

Although the weather was not favourable, there was a large turnout with many travelling from Falcon's native Norfolk. Amongst those present were the parents of both bride and groom, Viscountess Valentia, Lord and Lady Sudeley, Lady Birkbeck, Mr John Cator (High Sheriff of Norfolk), Mr E.G.Buxton (an important administrator in the history of Norfolk cricket) and a whole host of well-connected socialites. Whilst the gift from Norfolk C.C.C. was mentioned, none of Michael Falcon's team-mates were listed in the press as being present. It was probably a little too much of an upper-crust occasion for some of Norfolk's more rustic players, but one would have expected some of Falcon's more exalted chums such as Geoffrey Colman and Frank Mann to have been present. That they were actually in attendance and merely not listed by the press is a possibility.

---

30 Lyttelton played 57 first-class matches for Cambridge University and Middlesex. Alington was famously 'reprimanded' by Ted Wainwright, the old Yorkshire professional, for riding his bicycle across the outfield when he was headmaster of Shrewsbury School.

Chapter Five
At His Peak: 1919-1929

The Great War interrupted Michael Falcon's first-class and Minor Counties careers whilst they were at their height but, after his active service, he picked up as though there had been no hiatus and his starring years in the first-class game continued to around 1926, and in the Minor Counties Championship to around 1930.

In 1919 and the early 1920s, he was supporting himself as an MP – not thought of then as a full-time job – and to a lesser extent as a barrister, being able to juggle his Parliamentary and constituency duties with his cricketing commitments without upsetting more than his most demanding political opponents. Following his defeat in the 1923 election and his decision to leave politics he was obliged to seek a new career. A former colleague from the House of Commons, Edward Strauss,[31] made the suggestion that he take up the selling of hops for the Strauss family firm, one of the larger businesses in the hop 'market', based in Borough High Street just south of London Bridge. This might seem a little mundane a career for a man of Falcon's social standing, but it had the important feature that it was a business which largely took place in the autumn, thereby leaving plenty of time free for playing cricket in the summer. (According to his son, the brewers loved to talk cricket with Falcon when he made his 'rounds'.) He was not the first famous cricketer to enter the hop business. Alfred Mynn, the great Kent cricketer of the nineteenth century, had pre-dated Falcon in the trade; nor was he the last as the Kent wicket-keeper W.H.V. 'Hopper' Levett also became involved in a similar career in the 1930s. The drawback of hop-selling was that it obliged Falcon to leave his beloved Norfolk and he found himself based in Havering-atte-Bower, a rather suburban village near Romford in Essex, where he lived in another manor house, Bedfords, built in

---

31 Strauss was Liberal MP for Abingdon from 1906 to 1910, and then represented various Southwark constituencies as a National Liberal or Liberal between 1910 and 1940. He was a 'coupon' Liberal in the 1918 election, and in those particular hustings, therefore, 'on the same side' as Falcon. Like other farming-related businesses, the Strauss firm ran into financial difficulties in the 1930s.

1771, in its own sizeable landscaped grounds.[32] He was unable to undertake many of the behind-the-scenes, administrative tasks for which he later became known in Norfolk and he was also obliged to play some of his social cricket in his adopted county. *The Cricketer* magazine managed to track him down playing for Gidea Park in 1930, when he was obviously 'slumming it' as his figures showed: 46.3 overs, 20 maidens, 55 runs, 18 wickets and an average of 3.05. One of his team-mates was future Test star, Kenneth Farnes, whose 70 wickets were comparatively expensive at 8.07 each.

Rustic times for the Falcon family at Havering-atte-Bower in 1930.

Michael Falcon's sojourn in Essex came to an end in 1931, when he returned to Norfolk and a change in career, a move perhaps precipitated by the significant decline in the production of hops which occurred during the 1920s. By this time his first-class career had virtually come to an end, consisting by now only of the annual fixture between the Free Foresters and Cambridge University. As will be noted in Chapter Six, his role in the Norfolk team had also altered; by that date in that he was no longer by far the dominant

---

32   It was bought by Romford Borough Council in 1933 and its grounds made open to the public. After various uses the house was demolished in 1958.

figure in the side but merely just another man in an admittedly very good eleven.

It was whilst living in Essex that Falcon was first appointed a magistrate, thereby following in the family tradition. No doubt his legal experience qualified him admirably for the task. His status lapsed when he returned to Norfolk but he was reappointed in June 1934, and sat mainly in the area of east Norfolk in which he lived.

1919

After the Great War, the Minor Counties made no effort to organize a Championship before 1920. Norfolk attempted to run a festival in 1919, the secretary, Mr C.B.L.Prior, trying in vain to arrange matches with any of the neighbouring counties. In the end the festival consisted of a game versus a scratch Cambridge XI, a Club and Ground fixture against Fakenham and District and, thanks to the efforts of Michael Falcon at Lord's, a match was also arranged against MCC. Norfolk lost this by eight wickets, despite Falcon's fast bowling.

As he had no Minor Counties Championship to distract him, Falcon was able to play more first-class cricket than usual in 1919. He turned out in as many as seven games, including two against the Australian Imperial Forces (AIF) and three for the Gentlemen against the Players. His batting had fallen away by this point in his career (although there were later, sporadic glimpses of what he could do) and his bowling, although starting promisingly this year, came up against some solid batting from the Players. After taking 15 wickets in the first three innings in which he bowled, his final bag was a mere 25 wickets: a season's average of 23.48 was, however, satisfactory.

He started with nine cheap wickets, including the promising Donald Knight twice, for P.F.Warner's XI against Oxford University but finished on the losing side; despite that, his bowling received rave reviews, being described as 'really brilliant' in *The Times*, whilst the *Manchester Guardian* stated that he bowled better than figures of five for 67 would suggest. Then came the highlight of his season; selected for the Gentlemen of England against the AIF, he destroyed the Australians' batting with a fine display of fast swerve bowling. He took six for 41 and, with skipper Johnny Douglas contributing four for 34, bundled out the AIF for 85 and went on to win by an innings. Both *Wisden* and the *Guardian* made it clear that Michael Falcon was a more dangerous bowler on the day than Douglas, the Essex captain, whilst the *Daily Telegraph* described his action as 'practically perfect for a fast bowler'.

Playing for MCC against Yorkshire, Falcon started promisingly by dismissing Herbert Sutcliffe for six and David Denton and Roy Kilner for ducks, but then suffered some punishment from the Yorkshire lower order. A re-match with the AIF was his last game of the season: he didn't figure prominently as a bowler but helped to ensure a two-wicket win for C.I.Thornton's XI by blocking out whilst Wilfred Rhodes knocked off the ten runs needed for victory. All in all, not a bad season, excepting that his wickets against the Players cost him over 50 runs apiece.[33]

1920

The Minor Counties Championship made its reappearance, albeit in truncated form, and the all-rounder of the season was undoubtedly Michael Falcon. In a season of six games his performance was as pre-eminent as that of George Raikes in 1910. He scored 480 runs at an average of 60.00, including a career-best 205 against Hertfordshire (in which he hit two sixes and 20 fours in an innings characterised by his usual powerful driving), and took 46 wickets at 8.54 each (including 6 five-wicket returns). Unlike Raikes, however, Falcon was unable to guide Norfolk to the title as a couple of batting collapses resulted in defeats. In longer seasons to come Michael Falcon would score more runs and take more wickets, but 1920 marked the statistical summit of his dominance of the Minor Counties Championship. As well as his 205, he scored 134 against Essex II in an innings containing three sixes and 14 fours, described by the *Eastern Daily Press* as a 'brilliant display, driving with great power'.

With the ball it was also a story of almost uninterrupted success, with ten-wicket hauls against Bedfordshire and Hertfordshire: his two analyses of five for 39 against Bedfordshire on a lifeless wicket at Allen Park, Biddenham, stand out. Norfolk were operating with a two-man attack in 1920 as, apart from professional Harold

---

33 Luck was not with Falcon when bowling against the Players at Lord's (the most prestigious of the fixtures) as his fast bowling had no lesser batsmen than Jack Hobbs and George Gunn struggling to such a degree that their efforts were jeered by the crowd.

Watson, who took 39 cheap wickets, there was no other bowling to speak of.[34] Unsurprisingly, Falcon was invited to captain the Minor Counties XI in a two-day fixture against MCC, but the dates clashed with a Norfolk fixture, which naturally took precedence.

Norfolk being back in action, Falcon had less time to play first-class cricket but still managed to turn out for four matches. He had a successful season with the ball with one glaring exception. As in the previous year, he started with nine cheap wickets for the Free Foresters in a losing cause against Oxford University: this time the promising batsman he dismissed twice was Douglas Jardine. Again playing for the Free Foresters, he made a good start against Cambridge University, returning figures of six for 62, as he bowled the students out for 139. The *Daily Telegraph* said he bowled with 'deadly effect'. It was a vastly different story in the University's second innings as Hubert Ashton ran amok with a superb, unbeaten double century; a lot of them at the expense of Michael Falcon who returned figures of 23-2-145-2, probably the nadir of his career. Many runs were also conceded against the Players at The Oval, but Falcon was compensated by the capture of several wickets; with an analysis of five for 157 out of a total of 384, he justified his place in the fixture.

In March there was a meeting of Norfolk cricket clubs at which it was decided to form a Norfolk and Norwich Cricket Association. The aim was to help junior clubs keep in touch with the county authorities. Michael Falcon warmly commended the initiative to the floor, stating that he had consulted Lord Hawke about a similar set-up that operated in Yorkshire. He was unanimously elected the first President of the Association, an early example of his patient work behind the scenes for Norfolk cricket.

---

34   In his old age, when Harold Watson was asked his opinion on Michael Falcon's captaincy, the professional remarked wryly that his skipper would inspect the opposition's batting line-up before a match, and if he thought it weak, he would mentally prepare himself for a long bowl. If he thought it a more challenging proposition, he would 'allow' Harold plenty of work in his place. Perusal of match scorecards of the time reveals that there were occasions when Falcon bowled surprisingly few overs, given his status as the leader of the attack, but conversely there were also many matches in which he took his fair share of punishment. The most obvious example is that, when Surrey II racked up 550 for five declared at The Oval in June 1925, Falcon bowled more overs (32) than any other member of the Norfolk attack. That there was no lasting bad blood between the two strike bowlers is clear from Falcon's attendance at Watson's funeral in 1969, and from the extremely generous legacy left to the County Club by Watson's daughter, Vera. (I am grateful to Frank Devaney, who is Harold Watson's nephew, for this information.)

1921

The Minor Counties Championship was fully restored to its normal length for the 1921 season and, although he was unable to maintain the dominance of the previous campaign, Michael Falcon had another successful season, leading Norfolk from the front. With two centuries, he topped the batting averages and, with over 50 wickets, he finished second in the bowling list. He was a little erratic with the bat, his centuries in wins against Cambridgeshire and Bedfordshire being balanced with some low scores. With the ball he was competent rather than dangerous until he suddenly found form in the last two games of the season, dismissing twelve Kent II batsmen (albeit on that rarity in an otherwise dry season, a rain-affected wicket) and then nine Cambridgeshire batsmen in the last match.

It was in time for the 1921 season that Michael Falcon brought Jack Nichols back to play for the county of his birth. Nichols had played for Norfolk only briefly, in 1898, before his career as a professional cricketer took him away to Worcestershire and Staffordshire. He played five first-class games for the former county and made one appearance for the Minor Counties XI in 1912 but, by the end of the Great War, his time as a county cricketer appeared to be over. However Falcon, on his travels, visited Bishop's Stortford College, where he came across Nichols coaching the schoolboys. 'This,' Falcon declared, 'is the man we want for Norfolk.' Falcon duly poached him and Nichols repaid him by playing effectively as batsman, bowler and, when needed, wicket-keeper for the next ten years. After this he took on the role of coach until 1938, helping to bring on numerous players, including Bill Edrich.

Michael Falcon played in only two first-class games in 1921: that he finished on the winning side in both is the only similarity between them. In the first he and his fellow Free Foresters were thrashed all around The Parks by Oxford University's captain, 'Ronny' Holdsworth, who made a career-best double century. Falcon took three for 133 in only 26.5 overs as Oxford declared just shy of 400; in mitigation, *The Times* admitted that he was 'unlucky'. Although the Free Foresters saved the follow-on, their bowlers were put to the sword again as the students set up a declaration. Falcon leaked runs at more than six an over and his team were eventually set 420 to win in only 4 hours 30 minutes. At this point, Oxford looked odds-on victors and, at the very least, safe from defeat. However, all the Free Forester batsmen made runs and Michael Falcon, promoted from nine to five, extracted some measure of revenge for the damage done to his bowling by making an unbeaten 77. In partnership with Montagu Burrows, he put on an unbeaten 94 in just 50 minutes to carry his side to victory with thirty minutes to spare. Success with the bat was welcome, but his form with the ball against the University did not suggest that the next first-class match in which he played would be the one which would would place his name up there with, if not the all-time greats, then at least with the exceptionally gifted.

The story of the Archie MacLaren eleven's struggle to defeat the previously invincible 1921 Australians is well known. However, given the crucial role of Michael Falcon in the victory, it is necessary to examine it in some detail. The Australians, captained by Warwick Armstrong, overwhelmed England 5-0 in the 1920/21 Ashes series down under. Within months, now in England, they progressed round the country, defeating Test and county teams alike, often in just two days. Meanwhile, the ex-England skipper Archie MacLaren stated loudly and repeatedly that he could pick a side that would beat the Australians. When he was given his chance, in a fixture arranged at Eastbourne on 27, 29 and 30 August, his eleven featured none of the thirty players who appeared in the Tests. He selected an all-amateur eleven based upon the attacking batting and brilliant fielding of four players from Cambridge University: the brothers Ashton (Gilbert, Hubert and Claude) and Percy Chapman. Accurate, hostile bowling would hopefully be provided by Michael Falcon, Clem Gibson (also at Cambridge) and Walter Brearley, now 45 and a team-mate of MacLaren at Lancashire who played four Tests before the War.[35] The team was completed by wicket-keeper George Wood, who had only recently come down from Cambridge; ex-Oxford University batsman Geoffrey Foster; and Aubrey Faulkner, once a Test-class all-rounder for South Africa, but by now many years from his salad days and out of shape; and of course MacLaren himself, almost fifty.

On the big day, a large crowd of spectators and press gathered at The Saffrons Ground to see if the old-timer could make good on his promise to beat the Australians. MacLaren made a good start by winning the toss and electing to bat; but then it all went wrong.

---

35   Originally C.S. 'Father' Marriott, a spin bowler, was due to play, but he was unavailable and Walter Brearley was called upon.

Ted McDonald and Armstrong picked up five cheap wickets apiece as the England XI was bundled out for a humiliating 43 in only 20.1 overs.[36] Even worse was the news that Brearley had pulled a muscle and would be unable to bowl. How on earth would MacLaren fare, defending 43 with just three bowlers? The truth was that most of those present were too embarrassed to stay and witness the old man's discomfort. Nearly all the public and all the press, except Neville Cardus (who hero-worshipped MacLaren), drifted away.

It was now that MacLaren, who in his days as a Test captain was often a poor player-motivator, reacted superbly to adversity. Striding proudly onto the field of play at the head of his team, he made it clear that he was confident of eventual victory. At first things went even more awry as Gibson was not on-song and the Australians reached 80 for one. Having no alternative, MacLaren brought on Faulkner whose leg-breaks snaffled a couple of wickets. As if galvanised, Michael Falcon, who had been keeping up a barrage of hostile bowling, ran through the middle-order and tail-end, dismissing the Australians for just 174. According to *The Times*, Falcon was bowling faster than ever and Cardus in the *Manchester Guardian* described him as 'far better than our Test-match bowling' and 'an immense improvement on J.W.H.T.Douglas'. Falcon finished with figures of six for 67, being ably supported by Faulkner's four for 50.

The situation had improved somewhat but, not long into the next day, MacLaren's team were 60 for four and still on the road to defeat. At this point, Hubert Ashton was joined by Aubrey Faulkner and the fightback initiated by the bowling was taken up by the batting. Runs came freely and 154 was put on for the fifth wicket, until Ashton fell lbw to Armstrong for 75. Faulkner carried on to make 153 and the final total was 326. Falcon resisted gamely with the bat and helped Faulkner put on 51 for the eighth wicket.

Falcon and Gibson then resumed the attack, defending a target of 195. This time both bowlers were accurate and hostile and, with the help of the fielding from the Cambridge contingent, the Australians were made to fight for every run. Wickets began to fall and *The Times* stated 'The turning point of the game came when Mr Macartney was bowled by Mr. Falcon.' Macartney, nicknamed the 'Governor-General' because he liked to dominate the bowling,

---

36   Falcon's innings escaped Cardus' general condemnation of the batting in the *Manchester Guardian* which thought that he was 'the one man in the English side who managed a sound defence'.

was apparently so uncomfortable at being hemmed in by the accurate nature of the bowling and the superlative nature of the fielding that he played an impatient slash and missed a straight one. This was, however, Michael Falcon's last positive contribution to the match as (perhaps tiring) he suddenly lost his length, became expensive and had to be replaced by Faulkner. The South African proceeded to aid Gibson in running through the remainder of the Australians, leaving the England XI victorious by 28 runs.

Despite all his Test experience, it was undoubtedly one of the high points of Archie MacLaren's career, ranking alongside his first-class quadruple century against Somerset in 1895. Falcon and Gibson, with respectively eight and six wickets in the match, reached high points and their performances add to the debate as to whether they should have gone on to reach Test status (of which more below in Chapter Nine). Hubert Ashton's innings was

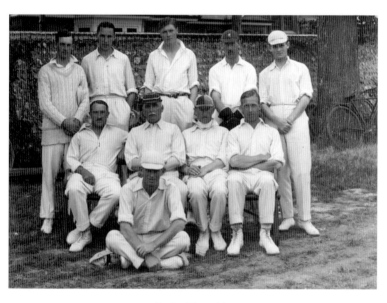

Against the odds.
The all-amateur 'England XI' which beat Warwick Armstrong's mighty Australians
at Eastbourne in August 1921.
Standing (l to r): G.Ashton, H.Ashton, A.P.F.Chapman, G.E.C.Wood (wk),
C.T.Ashton.
Seated: G.A.Faulkner, A.C.MacLaren (capt), G.N.Foster, M.Falcon.
On the ground: C.H.Gibson.
W.Brearley, injured on the first day, is missing.

similarly viewed in hindsight. As for the chief architect of victory, Faulkner, he already had sufficient on his *curriculum vitae* to make this just another achievement, albeit a highly significant one.

Rumour has it that the Australians had a lucky mascot which resided in their dressing rooms all through the tour but which was mysteriously absent during this defeat and the subsequent, second reverse. This may be a bit of a myth but it is certain that the tourists treated this match seriously and that the defeated captain's comments on his reverse were unprintable.

1922

If the 1920 season was the highlight of Michael Falcon's career as an all-rounder in Minor Counties circles when viewed in terms of averages, then the 1922 season, by virtue of being the longest in which he played, was the pinnacle when examined using aggregates as a benchmark. Appearing in all fourteen Norfolk matches, he scored no fewer than 728 runs and took 72 wickets. He averaged nearly 35 with the bat and was part of a highly effective bowling attack in which five bowlers took 27 or more wickets each, all at an average of less than 16. Walter Beadsmoore was the most economical, his 40 victims costing a mere 10.40 each. Falcon also took twelve catches, his highest bag for a season.

Michael Falcon scored steadily throughout the season, the highlight being his century, an innings of 113, which helped Norfolk to a four-wicket win over old rivals Staffordshire who would soon be replaced by Buckinghamshire as the 'needle' opponents in the Championship. The innings took just over two hours and was, like most of his big innings, characterised by its superb driving. He could hook too, as he showed in an innings of 95 in just under two hours against Hertfordshire. His bowling successes were spread through the season and enthusiastic quotes from the *Eastern Daily Press* seem to indicate that he was at his fiercest and best: ' ... and Falcon at his best is an England bowler'; 'Falcon quickly got rid of him ... with a terrific delivery, knocking his stumps clean out of the ground'; 'Falcon bowled very fast'; 'the Norfolk captain bowling at a tremendous pace'; and 'with a breeze behind him, Falcon bowled at a great pace'.

With all the bowlers firing and the batting being at least competent, the Norfolk side had an excellent season, winning eight matches outright and taking first-innings points in the other four.

Unsurprisingly they finished top of the Minor Counties Championship table and were challenged by runners-up Buckinghamshire. In the 'play-off' at Lakenham, Buckinghamshire batted first but, largely due to a fine innings of 98 by Geoffrey Colman, Norfolk conceded a first-innings lead of just seven runs. When Norfolk's attack, headed by Falcon with four for 18, skittled Buckinghamshire for just 90 in their second innings, victory looked a certainty. Unfortunately the Norfolk top-order collapsed, so that when Falcon and Richard Carter came together the score was 39 for five. They increased the score to 81, whereupon a further four wickets fell without addition, and Buckinghamshire eventually triumphed by eight runs, with the bowling honours going to spinner Frank Edwards who took eleven wickets in the match. It may have been an anticlimactic end to the season but the *Eastern Daily Press* was still prompted to flights of fancy with the headline: 'Should Norfolk Be A First-Class County?' In the end the paper decided that, sadly, there was an insufficient fan base to support first-class cricket in the county.[37] The Challenge Match drew crowds of over 2,000, but attendances were much smaller for less important games.

Whilst ambitions for first-class status were never met, Norfolk do seem, however, to have been one of the more important of the Minor Counties for, with the exception of the Australians and the 1936 Indians, they were awarded prestigious fixtures against all the touring sides from 1927 until the Second World War. To what extent this reflects Norfolk's position as a 'senior' second-class county *per se* and how much it was due to Michael Falcon using his position on the MCC Committee to ensure that touring teams would make regular trips to Lakenham is unclear. He certainly valued these games highly as he was known to stress publicly the importance of maintaining high-quality pitches in the county in

---

37   It was nearly forty years since the *Eastern Daily Press* had last campaigned for Norfolk to be granted first-class status. In the mid-1880s the county was certainly strong on paper, with the batting anchored by the skipper and old Cambridge Blue, Kerry Jarvis, and a varied and penetrative bowling attack. Unfortunately the most skilled amateurs were not always available. More importantly, just as in the 1920s, the public were not interested in significant numbers to make first-class cricket a viable proposition. Crowds in the region of just 300 were noted in the *Eastern Daily Press* reports of the time, which contrast with the attendance of over 4,000 spectators who attended Norfolk's visit to Northamptonshire in 1883. (The ACS has – in more recent times – classified six Norfolk matches played between 1820 and 1836 as first-class.)

order that the tourists might continue to visit Norfolk.[38]

Norfolk were actually beaten a second time in 1922, and it was a comprehensive thrashing by 138 runs, in early August, at the hands of the Eton Ramblers, a side with six players who had played first-class cricket. Michael Falcon did very well with the ball, taking five for 58 and seven for 37, but his failure to score more than one run in two innings was probably the difference between the two teams.

Falcon was also involved in Parliamentary cricket this year, captaining the 'North' against the 'South' in a House of Commons 'trial match' which purported to aid the selectors of the newly resuscitated Parliamentary Cricket Association. He bowled only two overs and batted last so was hardly inconvenienced, but later turned out for the Lords and Commons team defeated by Westminster School. Uncharacteristically for this season, his 18 overs went unrewarded but he saved face by top-scoring with an innings of 44.

At the end of the cricket season Falcon showed a side of him seldom seen elsewhere. Attending the annual dinner of the Horning and District Cricket Club, of which he was president, he was called on for a song and gave 'Hearts of Oak', leading the company in a rousing chorus. As an encore he sang 'Soldiers of the King' which was another triumph. Although he was, by upbringing, a Tory grandee he was no snob and was happy to mix with anyone who shared his passion for cricket in general and for Norfolk cricket in particular.

1923

If the local press thought Norfolk worthy of first-class status based on their results of 1922, then the results of the 1923 season would have been enough to disillusion them swiftly. Defeated three times, Norfolk slipped to sixteenth in a table of twenty. It wasn't the fault of their skipper as he led the way with 678 runs, including six scores of over fifty, and 54 wickets. He started well with the bat, making 98 against Hertfordshire and continued in

---

38   After the Second World War Norfolk were no longer considered worthy of fixtures with touring teams in their own right, but for a couple of years they were awarded 'second prize' in that Lakenham played host to the matches between the Minor Counties representative XI and the 1951 South Africans and the 1952 Indians. Unlike the game against South Africa in 1924 however, Norfolk players found it hard to gain selection for these fixtures.

fine form all season. Likewise, with the ball, Hertfordshire and Bedfordshire were made to suffer early on but the highlight of the season was a haul of eight for 41 against Bedfordshire at Lakenham. With no support coming from his team-mates, his spell was in vain as Bedfordshire won comfortably.

Whilst conceding that Falcon might have been a little faster ten years previously, the local press provides evidence that he was still a very quick bowler at the Minor Counties level, especially when armed with the new ball. Often bowling to four or five slips, he had trouble finding a wicket-keeper who could take him comfortably and in the end Jack Nichols had to don the gloves. Had Falcon been possessed of the fast bowler's hostility of purpose towards the batsmen, he could have been positively dangerous but he preferred to pitch it up and dismiss the batsmen with his swerve. As a result injuries were scarce: they did, however, happen now and again and against Kent II a shorter length ball rose 'and hit the tall Claud Douglas on the side of the head and the batsman went down. The sound of the impact could be heard all over the field.'

The tourists in 1923 were the West Indians. Early in their tour they met a not particularly strong MCC team but, replying to a total of only 228, they struggled to 121 for eight before rain brought the match to a close. Michael Falcon was their chief tormentor with the ball, taking three for 38. In his annual game for the Free Foresters against Cambridge University Falcon met with extremely mixed fortunes. Responding to a total of 420, the University were bowled out for 306, Falcon taking six for 76 in 31 accurate overs. The Free Foresters eventually declared leaving a target of 375 – which the University comfortably made for the loss of only three wickets in a mere 75 overs. The Norfolk captain's 19 overs went wicketless and leaked 113 runs.[39] This was a low point which almost matched his two for 145 against the University in 1920. Despite this clobbering, Falcon was invited to represent the Gentlemen at The Oval; although his four wickets were not cheap he held his own in dismissing Jack Hobbs (twice), William Whysall and Wally Hammond and received a favourable review in the *Manchester Guardian*.

The season was rounded off socially with a dance held in connection with the Norfolk C.C.C. at the Arlington Rooms in Norwich. There were about 150 guests who danced into the early

---

39   In one over Tom Lowry hit him for one six and three fours.

hours. The dance organising committee included Michael Falcon, Geoffrey Colman, Walter Beadsmoore and Geoffrey Stevens.

This is perhaps the right place to cover a further story illustrating Falcon's concern for grassroots cricket, though it may have political undertones. In March 1923, it was announced that the MP for East Norfolk was to present a cricket challenge cup for village clubs in the area of his constituency, starting at the commencement of the next cricket season. To be known as the Falcon Cup, this competition took its place alongside the large number of other trophies on offer in Norfolk, most of them organised on a local basis.

In the first year of the Falcon Cup the competition was organised in two divisions, the top teams in the two mini-leagues meeting in a final. In one division Martham finished unbeaten, triumphing over Ingham, Horning & District Reserves, Happisburgh and Hoveton Reserves, whilst in the other Langley Park & Loddon were similarly undefeated in a division including Ditchingham, Berg Apton and Haddiscoe.

The final was held at the Norwich Union Fire Office Ground and, despite the fact that the wicket was reported as 'good', the scores were very low. Langley Park & Loddon batted first and amassed a feeble 36; however, this was comfortably enough as Martham were dismissed for a miserable 28. It had been a good year for Langley Park & Loddon who were only beaten once all season and that was in the final of the Norfolk Junior Cup, where Mattishall proved too strong for them. The match was originally intended for a Saturday, but had to be switched to midweek which meant that Michael Falcon couldn't be present to give away his own trophy: his wife, Kathleen, stood in for him and handed the cup to Mr A.Bentley, the winning captain. Following the presentation the players and their families were entertained to tea provided at Michael Falcon's expense.

By the next season Falcon was no longer the local MP. However, he showed that the Cup was no cynical, vote-winning device by continuing to support the competition. Unfortunately, the number of clubs participating fell away in the years following 1923 and the format of a single league was adopted. Tables headed 'Falcon League Cup' and match results continued to appear sporadically in the local press until the late 1930s. Its history, now forgotten, is an example of the interest Michael Falcon took in local cricket, even at its lowest levels and the lengths to which he would go to foster its development.

1924

Norfolk had another mediocre season in the wet summer of 1924 but, as with the previous season, it wasn't due to lack of success from their captain who again led from the front. He scored 580 runs in ten completed innings and added another 45 wickets to his Minor Counties career total. The highlight of his season was an all-round *tour de force* against Surrey II at Hunstanton: first he took seven for 37, with notable command of break and swerve, which led to the dismissal of Surrey for a mere 102. Then he racked up 148 with strokes all round the wicket, and finally finished with four for 41 as Surrey subsided by an innings. Staffordshire also suffered from the effects of Michael Falcon's batting but they were unlucky in that, having forced Norfolk to follow on 156 behind, largely due to Sydney Barnes taking seven for 38, the great bowler (now 51) promptly pulled a muscle. Falcon took full advantage with a solidly compiled, unbeaten 129, thereby saving the match. Bowling, he took three more five-wicket hauls in addition to his success against Surrey II, but he was the cause of another injury as, against Staffordshire, one of his fastest balls rose steeply from the pitch, hit John Johnson on the jaw and laid him out.

Successful though his Minor Counties season had been, it was in his three first-class games that Michael Falcon's reputation was significantly augmented. His first appearance was for H.D.G.Leveson Gower's XI against the touring South Africans at Reigate. He took but two expensive wickets, but it was his batting in the second innings which proved to be crucial. Coming in at nine with little to follow and 34 still needed to win, he nervelessly helped Emmott Robinson knock off the runs in 20 minutes, his share being an unbeaten 12. Only a couple of days later Falcon made, for him, the unusual choice to play for the Gentlemen at The Oval rather than for Norfolk. The Players' opening batsmen, Jack Hobbs and Andy Sandham, added 129 runs before lunch, but after the break Falcon bowled at his finest, taking seven for 78 and being largely responsible for the dismissal of the Players for just 288. Philip Trevor in the *Daily Telegraph* reported: 'His performance was all the better seeing that before he got anyone out there was every possibility that no bowler would do even moderately well.' 'Plum' Warner, always a fan, added, 'Falcon was in his best form.

He kept up a fine pace, and was always making the ball rise at an awkward height, and the ball off which Strudwick was caught at short slip might have got out the greatest batsman in England so abruptly did it rise from the pitch.' The *Manchester Guardian* described Falcon as having 'bowled superbly'. Unfortunately the Gentlemen were unable to take advantage of Falcon's bowling and had to follow on: Falcon soon found himself whipping in for the second time to join Arthur Gilligan in a seemingly hopeless cause. Gilligan greeted the appearance of Falcon by launching a calculated assault on the Players' attack so severe that 134 runs were added for the tenth wicket in only 70 minutes. Playing very much a supporting role, Falcon made an unbeaten 34 in a record tenth-wicket partnership for the Gentlemen. *The Times*, the *Telegraph* and 'Plum' Warner (again) were all favourably impressed by his innings. It remains a bit of a mystery why he 'lost' his batting to some extent at the first-class level whilst remaining one of the premier performers with the willow in the Minor Counties game.[40] (He did, of course, show sporadic glimpses of what he could do with the bat in first-class fixtures in the twenties.) Gilligan was eventually dismissed for 112,[41] but the earlier ineptitude of the Gentlemen meant that the Players were able to coast home by six wickets. Still, it was one of the highlights of Falcon's first-class career.

Michael Falcon's third first-class match of the season was, if anything, even more of a highlight than the match at The Oval; up there with his performance for Archie MacLaren's side at Eastbourne in 1921. He was chosen to captain a Minor Counties XI against the South Africans, in a fixture awarded first-class status, and led his team to victory in front of his home crowd at Lakenham. Whilst it is true that, as opponents, the South Africans were vastly inferior to Armstrong's tourists, they treated the Minor Counties XI with respect and put out a near Test-strength side. What made the game so special for Falcon and the Norfolk

---

40 An interesting theory was put forward by Mohammad Nissar – himself a fast bowler of great reputation who started life as a batsman. He stated that 'I feel that a fast bowler gradually loses the capacity to use his bat with skill, the reason being that the arm muscles of a bowler – especially the fast one – are developed in such a manner that the flexibility and pliancy which are required for the execution of a good stroke are lost.' Nissar's hypothesis may have seemed plausible in the 1930s for there had been few pace-bowling all-rounders in the first-class game up to his day but there have been so many examples since that his idea no longer holds water.

41 Gilligan's effort with the bat, having been hit over the heart in the first innings, was thought to have had a permanent effect on his ability to bowl fast. He never bowled with his old hostility again after this match.

spectators alike was that no fewer than seven members of the Minor Counties eleven were Norfolk players, appearing in front of their home crowd. This favouring of one county was something of a rarity as teams for Minor Counties representative games were generally selected from all across the country. The Norfolk players were Falcon himself, Geoffrey Colman, Geoffrey Stevens, Walter Beadsmoore, John Coldham, Guy Pedder and Harold Watson. The four 'given men' (as they would have been described in olden days) were genuine stars at the Minor Counties level. They were Charles Titchmarsh, the master batsman from Hertfordshire; Percy Chapman, a team-mate of Falcon at Eastbourne in 1921, who was still with Berkshire but would soon be captain of the England Test team; Alexander Doggart, a solid batsman who represented Durham; and Hertfordshire's Jack Meyer, an off-break bowler and competent bat, who was still up at Cambridge but who had a long first-class career in India and Somerset ahead of him.

Michael Falcon won the toss and decided to bat, but the Minor Counties didn't fare too well and it took a defiant 40 from the aggressive Coldham, undoubtedly the highpoint of his career, to guide his team to a total of 196. The South Africans collapsed in turn before the spin of Meyer, who bowled unchanged to take six for 60 whilst Falcon, 'bowling at a great pace,' supported him with three for 48, leaving the Minor Counties with a first innings lead of 47. On the second day the 'guest' batsmen pulled their weight:

Michael Falcon leads out the Minor Counties side against the South Africans at Lakenham, 1924.

Titchmarsh scored 80 and put on 104 for the fourth wicket with Chapman whose contribution was 68. Over 3,000 spectators were present to see the South Africans set a total of 320; they reached a promising 66 for the loss of one wicket before rain stopped play at 6.15 pm on the second day.

On the final day Michael Falcon bowled like a Trojan, with, at first, little support from his team-mates. He captured the first five wickets to fall, including the famous batsmen Dave Nourse and Herbie Taylor. However, he bowled himself to a standstill and, at 257 for six, the South Africans looked to have saved the game. Falcon turned to slow left-armer Walter Beadsmoore for one last effort and he responded by claiming a wicket immediately, but the South Africans made a further stand and the Minor Counties chance appeared to have gone. Suddenly Beadsmoore struck gold and took the remaining three wickets in 13 balls to secure a win by 25 runs, with but two minutes to spare. In his only first-class game Beadsmoore took four for 53 and, like Coldham, this match was the high point of his career.

Michael Falcon, with second innings figures of five for 103, has not received sufficient credit for his sterling work as captain and strike bowler in a major upset and a magnificent result. Perhaps there were too many Norfolk players involved for most Minor County observers to be interested, but given the Norfolk-based flavour of the victory, it's a fair bet that Michael Falcon would have been immensely proud of his team.

1925

Norfolk's season was encouraging with five wins and only one defeat. In contrast to previous seasons Michael Falcon did not dominate proceedings, but was one of a group of leading players, all of whom contributed significantly to Norfolk's cause. Four players topped 400 runs and averaged over 30 with the bat: Geoffrey Stevens, Geoffrey Colman, Jack Nichols and Falcon, whilst four players also took 28 or more wickets and averaged under 20 with the ball: Walter Beadsmoore, Harold Watson, Jack Nichols and Falcon. The skipper finished as low as fourth in both batting and bowling averages, but was the leading wicket taker, in a season which for him has to be rated a little below par. He made an excellent start with the bat, rattling up 136 in 150 minutes against Leicestershire II in a knock which contained two sixes and

14 fours and which set up an innings victory, but after that he fell away and failed to pass 50 for the rest of the season. With the ball he twice achieved five-wicket returns against Hertfordshire, but the highlight of the season was undoubtedly the match against Staffordshire at Lakenham – a fixture still being described by the *Eastern Daily Press* as being akin to a Roses match in the intensity of its rivalry. Falcon won the toss and gambled by putting Staffordshire in. Bowling in-swingers (a new weapon in his armoury) he was mainly responsible for shooting out the visitors for a mere 105, taking six for 33. Norfolk then successfully saw off Sydney Barnes and went on to win by ten wickets. Fast inswingers were also seen to trouble the batsmen (and the wicket-keeper) against Kent II at Lakenham. At 37 years of age, Falcon was still employing new tricks and was still able to work up a fair pace when conditions were suitable.

In June Falcon found time to skipper the Minor Counties North against the Minor Counties South, captained by Walter Franklin. It turned out to be one of his most erratic performances. Opening the batting, he failed twice and his figures of one for 89 (conceded in just 16.3 overs) in the South's first innings of just 255 compared unfavourably with those of the other bowlers in his attack. In complete contrast, he fired out seven of the first eight batsmen in the South's second innings and was largely responsible for their collapse to 124 all out in only 30 overs, a comprehensive victory being his reward.

His first-class season was restricted to his annual appearance for the Free Foresters against Cambridge University and was an all-round triumph for the Norfolk captain. After the Free Foresters collapsed to 95 all out, Falcon replied by taking five for 65 to restrict the University to 193.[42] Batting at four, he then top-scored

---

42 This was Falcon's last five-wicket innings return in first-class cricket, and this is perhaps the right place to draw attention to the 'clustering' of his wicket-taking. He took 231 first-class wickets, of which 112 (48.5%) came in innings where he took five or more. This percentage puts him in the same 'range' as many top-quality spinners, for example, Charlie Parker (51.7%); 'Charlie' Blythe (51.5%); Hedley Verity (51.5%); Tom Goddard (51.1%) and Johnny Clay (46.5%), and considerably higher than most Test class pace bowlers, such as Harold Larwood (39.0%); Richard Hadlee (38.5%); Alec Bedser (27.9%) and Ray Lindwall (24.1%). Admittedly, Falcon appeared far less frequently than all these others and the range of players sampled for this survey was not comprehensive, but his high percentage appears to be genuinely noteworthy for a quick bowler. It seems likely that he scores highly because he was both genuinely capable of deadly spells even against the very best when 'on song' and also erratic, being expensive on 'off' days. The clustering of wickets was less pronounced in his Minor Counties career, where 42.2% of his wickets came in hauls of five wickets or more.

with 77 as the Free Foresters' upper order flourished. This was not one of Falcon's best innings; both *The Times* and the *Manchester Guardian* remarked that he was fortunate. A decent target was set and 'Father' Marriott, with figures of seven for 40 on a wicket now taking spin, ensured that Cambridge, who mustered only 152, went down to a 19-run defeat, their first loss of the season.

In October, Michael Falcon was given a ringing endorsement by no less a player than Jack Hobbs,[43] who was at the peak of his fame, having passed W.G.Grace's record number of first-class centuries earlier in the year. Visiting Norwich, he spoke at the Agricultural Hall Assembly Rooms, under the auspices of the YMCA, to an audience which included Geoffrey Colman and Geoffrey Stevens, who heard him praise the bowling of Johnny Douglas, Charlie Blythe, Ted Arnold and Sydney Barnes, before turning to Falcon. Referring to the match between Lionel Robinson's XI and the Australians at Old Buckenham in 1921, Hobbs said: 'I cannot understand why, in that match, we had not on our side one of Norfolk's most talented cricketers, a gentleman whose aid would be welcome to any first-class county. I refer to Mr Michael Falcon – (applause) – a gentleman in every sense of the word, and a fast bowler of great merit.' Hobbs went on to say that Falcon's performances for the Gentlemen against the Players made one regret that he had been lost to the first-class game.

1926

The Australians arrived in 1926 and, although they looked strong in the first-class arena, they were still cannon-fodder for Michael Falcon when they met the Minor Counties at Maidenhead in the tour-opener. The two-day match was not awarded first-class status and the Australians were not able to get in much useful practice as there was no play on the first day due to rain and the second day was also truncated. The first three wickets fell to other bowlers but then, just after lunch, Falcon had Warren Bardsley stumped by Franklin with the score at 99. From then on, although *Wisden* described the turf as 'sodden' and 'too slow to give bowlers much help', he was far too cunning for batsmen not used to English conditions. He took the last seven wickets, including a spell of four wickets in five overs for just nine runs and finished with figures of

---

43   Perhaps not surprisingly. As can be seen in the statistical appendix at the end of this book, Falcon had made dismissing Hobbs something of a speciality.

The 1926 Minor Counties v Australians match at Lakenham.
Players and officials wait for the official photographer, with Falcon seated fifth
from the right.

'In deck-chair's gentle curve.'
This Norfolk side of 1927 won only one of its ten Championship matches.
This particular line-up is for the home fixture against Hertfordshire at the
beginning of August.
Standing (l to r): B.W.Rought-Rought, E.C.Williamson (wk), R.C.Rought-Rought,
J.E.Nichols, H.F.Low, R.J.Covill, H.Watson.
Seated: J.M Coldham, G.R.R.Colman, M.Falcon (capt), G.A.Stevens,
W.A.Beadsmoore.

seven for 42. Only Jack Ryder with an unbeaten 43 looked at all comfortable as Falcon's victims included Bill Woodfull and Bill Ponsford, batsmen who would become famous as all-time greats. *The Cricketer* correspondent commented that 'he bowled admirably. He has shortened his run up to the wicket, and he accommodated his pace to the slow pitch. He is, we should say, a more subtle bowler than formerly, for he imparts to his deliveries rather more variety of pace. Falcon is 38, but he is ten years younger in physical fitness, and his record against Australian teams is notable ... determination and splendid physique squeezed every bit of pace that there was to be had out of a lifeless wicket.' The Australians were eventually dismissed for 179 and there was only time for the Minor Counties XI to make 115 for four in reply.

Norfolk had a disastrous time in the Minor Counties Championship, being defeated five times in ten matches and failing to win even a single fixture. It was not the fault of Michael Falcon, who headed both the batting and bowling averages. Falcon's 672 runs were scored consistently through the season with one century and seven half-centuries – his most fifties in a season. Scores of 56 and 107 not out against Kent II at Chatham were the highlight, his driving being as prominent as usual.

With the ball, Falcon's total of 37 wickets at 19.35 was steady rather than spectacular, but all the other bowlers were failures. However signs of his age, quite advanced for a fast bowler, were now becoming visible at the Minor Counties level as well as at Maidenhead. Although it was reported that, against Kent II, 'he bowled very fast, kept an excellent length, and made the ball do something in the air', when Hertfordshire visited Lakenham the paper noted that his 'run up to the wicket is now much shorter and his pace not so fast as formerly.' However, swing away from the bat was still in evidence and he obtained four five-wicket returns. A rare setback at this level occurred in the home fixture against Hertfordshire when Charles Titchmarsh made a splendid 218. Falcon went wicketless for 82 runs, although he did have Titchmarsh dropped by Jack Nichols in the slips[44] when the batsmen had scored only 23. He was hooked to distraction by the 'little master' as reported by Eric Edrich:

---

44   *Wisden* was particularly critical of the Norfolk's fielding this season, reporting it as 'the outstanding cause of the county's lack of success'.

He was only a little fellow and he was hooking Michael Falcon off his eyebrows. First he hit him to square-leg, and when they moved fine-leg round he started hitting him fine. When he got to 200 we were all cheering madly when a pigeon landed on the wicket, and Titchmarsh somehow got it to hop on to his bat. He held it up to the crowd to acknowledge the cheering, then sent it flapping off with a flick of the wrist. I thought the cheering would never stop.

Charles Titchmarsh was one of the very few batsmen in the Minor Counties Championship who was equal to the task of facing Michael Falcon at his best. He was as pre-eminent a batsman in Hertfordshire as Falcon was in Norfolk as an all-rounder. Like Falcon, he could certainly have played first-class county cricket had he been so minded. He did find time to participate in Archie MacLaren's 1922/23 tour of Australia and New Zealand and, in all first-class cricket, scored 2,589 runs at a highly creditable average of 39.22.

Michael Falcon managed to squeeze four first-class matches into a very full season. Indeed he was so busy that he had to miss Norfolk's last Championship fixture as he had business to attend to in London.[45] A strong MCC side, led by Falcon, who did little, were saved by rain when playing against the tourists. Playing against Cambridge University for the Free Foresters, he conceded 124 runs in taking three first innings wickets[46] but then redeemed himself with an undefeated innings of 86, his highest first-class score since his century for MCC against Leicestershire in 1911. He also did little for the Gentlemen either at The Oval or at Scarborough and his first-class career outside of his annual appearance for the Free Foresters at Fenner's appeared to be winding down; his four first-class wickets were taken at a cost of over 80 runs apiece.

Not to be outshone, Falcon's wife Kathleen also played cricket in 1926. An article in the *Norfolk News* reported that she took part in a ladies' match, making nine and one and taking a single wicket. As

---

45 In the ten seasons from 1920 to 1929, Falcon played 24 three-day first-class matches, 99 two-day matches for Norfolk and often appeared in one or two other important two-day matches per season. Typically he was thus playing 'senior cricket' on about thirty days a season, to which should be added say three or four days for travelling to or returning from fixtures well away from his home.

46 Falcon again found himself being hit for 18 in an over by a Cambridge undergraduate; this time Jack Meyer was the batsman.

will be reported later, she was not the last female to represent the Falcon family on the cricket field for her daughter, Sybil, was a keen player.

1927

Though *Wisden* grumbled again about the county's 'seldom above moderate' fielding, Norfolk had a vastly improved showing following their disastrous season in 1926, being defeated only three times, twice by their new arch-rivals Buckinghamshire and also by New Zealand, and recording one win, against Leicestershire II. This recovery, which put them in mid-table in the Minor Counties competition, was not due to an improved team batting performance. Only Michael Falcon, with over 500 runs at an average of nearly 40, scored runs on any scale. If anything, the rest of the batting was even poorer than that in 1926. Falcon's batting was somewhat inconsistent, but he did register two centuries, against Hertfordshire and Kent II, noted, as usual, for his powerful driving. The improvement in the team's performance was due to a recovery in the bowling, Walter Beadsmoore particularly starring with 35 wickets at an average of under 10.

Michael Falcon took only 28 wickets (but at a reasonable average of under 20) and it was noticeable that he bowled fewer overs than usual. He did have his day of success with the ball against Buckinghamshire, at High Wycombe where he employed what for him was a novel method of attack: 'Falcon bowled round the wicket with only three fieldsmen on the off-side of the wicket, and the batsmen had difficulty in keeping the ball away from three short-leg fielders. At one point Falcon bowled seven overs for 16 runs and four wickets.' And again: 'Falcon bowled finely to take five wickets in the innings for 57 runs and was so successful with the leg-theory that he bowled for more overs at a stretch than usual.' As he aged, Michael Falcon became more and more versatile. After relying almost exclusively on pace at Harrow, he developed his highly effective outswinger before the Great War; then he developed the inswinger in 1925 and now he was backing up that inswing with a leg-theory field in the style of Fred Root, the Worcestershire medium pacer.

Falcon took place in a record-breaking match when playing for MCC against the New Zealanders. No fewer than 1,502 runs were scored, in 332.3 six-ball overs, for the loss of just 28 wickets, which was then a record for a three-day first-class fixture in England. Falcon shared his unimpressive match figures – two for 107 off 17 overs – with most other bowlers in the game.

The 1927 season was the setting for Michael Falcon's last hurrah for the Gentlemen. Playing at The Oval, he was the fifth bowler to be called on and returned figures of four for 60, highly creditable given that the Players declared at 424 for nine. The Gentlemen had to follow on and, in the second innings, Falcon and his deadly Buckinghamshire rival, Walter Franklin, combined to add an unbeaten 29 for the ninth wicket, so holding out for a draw.[47]

1928

Norfolk started their campaign in 1928 against the West Indians at Lakenham. Although Falcon took but one wicket in his twenty overs, he conceded only 27 runs and, at forty years of age, showed he was still capable of bowling at pace. *The Times* stated: 'Falcon bowled one over to Browne which made one understand why he is a pace bowler the Australians dislike. Every ball beat the batsman by that pace off the pitch which, whatever the fashion of swing and swerve may be, remains the one infallible sign of a good bowler.'

The county's performance in the Minor Counties Championship continued to improve, with three wins and only one defeat. Following on his good showing against the tourists, Falcon bowled splendidly and took 43 wickets at just over 15 apiece. His best performances were against Buckinghamshire: he took seven for 82 (including a hat-trick) at Ascott Park, near Wing, and 13 wickets in the last match of the season at Lakenham, being largely responsible for a rare victory against Walter Franklin's men. He topped the side's batting averages, making the only two centuries scored by Norfolk all summer, against Surrey II and Buckinghamshire (at Ascott Park), and scoring nearly 200 runs more than the second most prolific bat, Rodney Rought-Rought. Facing a Surrey II score of 416, Falcon put on 213 for the third wicket with Harry Low, making his usual quota of powerful drives. As well as his performance at Ascott Park, another all-round display of note took place at Lakenham against Leicestershire II when he scored 98 and took six for 28.

---

47   Falcon and Franklin held out for the last 30, 35 or 45 minutes: the broadsheets all give different durations!

At the end of the season Falcon received an enthusiastic review in the *Eastern Daily Press*: 'Michael Falcon, who once again heads the batting and bowling averages had brilliant days when he almost carried the rest of the side on his shoulders.'

1929

Michael Falcon continued to thrive with the bat in 1929. The highlight was an innings of 189 against Leicestershire II at Hinckley, his second highest ever for Norfolk. He hit three sixes and 29 fours and added 170 in 67 minutes for the sixth wicket with John Bally, his driving being described as 'superb'. Leicestershire II put up little fight and lost by an innings, Falcon taking five for 50 in their first knock. For the rest of the year he was consistent rather than spectacular with both bat and ball, and in a season dominated by Rodney Rought-Rought's haul of 59 wickets, his bag of 29 was more expensive than those of all the other regular bowlers. He did, though, perform well against his old foe, the South Africans, taking three for 65 at Lakenham. He also faced the South Africans representing MCC in his last first-class fixture against a touring side, picking up a couple of wickets.

Players and officials in the Norfolk v South Africans match at Lakenham in June 1929.
Back row (l to r): H.G.Owen-Smith, B.W.Rought-Rought, E.L.Dalton.
Standing: H.B.Cameron, H.F.Low, J.H.Bally, A.J.Bell, W.A.Beadsmoore, W.McMillan, R.C.Rought-Rought, G.A.Stevens, R.H.Gladden, A.L.Ochse.
Seated: J.A.Christy, J.E.Nichols, H.W.Taylor, S.Christopherson (Norfolk President), M.Falcon, H.O.Frielinghaus (SA manager), C.L.Vincent, B.Mitchell.
On the ground: F.R.Bell, G.N.Scott-Chad, E.A.Van der Merwe.

Chapter Six
Elder Statesman: 1930-1939

In the period between 1912 and 1929 Michael Falcon had been as dominant in his team as any performer in the Minor Counties Championship, equalling such outstanding players as Sydney Barnes of Staffordshire and Charles Titchmarsh of Hertfordshire. He led from the front with both bat and ball and often shone in the field as well. However, by 1931 he was 43 years old and his period of pre-eminence was coming to an end. There were to be no more centuries, although he would register a further 22 half-centuries in the Championship. Though he would still pick up wickets at vital times whilst bowling at a reduced pace, he could no longer seize a game and turn it around on his own. At the same time his team-mates from the 1920s were retiring. Harold Watson played his last game in 1927; Geoffrey Stevens and Geoffrey Colman both retired in 1930; whilst Walter Beadsmoore and Jack Nichols soldiered on until 1931. In such circumstances, most skippers would have been content to slip quietly away, but Michael Falcon was not an ordinary leader. He was still exceptionally fit, and thus able to contribute to Norfolk's team as what we would now call a 'bits-and-pieces' player, playing a supporting role with both bat and ball where needed.[48]

The 1930s turned out to be another 'Golden Age' of Norfolk cricket, echoing back to the first just before the Great War. The influx of talent from Oxford and Cambridge Universities and from the Edrich family led to the formation of a team which, although it never won the title, regularly finished high in the table and, from August 1932 to July 1937, went 41 Championship matches undefeated. Michael Falcon presided over this 'Golden Age' with benevolence. Unlike his contemporary and sparring partner at

---

48   The decline in Falcon's ability with the bat was reflected in a change in his place in Norfolk's batting order. In the first part of his career he generally appeared at between three and five in the order, other than in 1911, 1920 and 1923 when he usually opened the batting. From 1926, a preference for four became increasingly apparent until the middle of the 1934 season when he dropped down to six, a position he held for virtually every match until his retirement.

Buckinghamshire, Walter Franklin, who was a martinet whose desperate will-to-win led him to terrorize young players, Falcon was on extremely friendly terms with his fellow amateurs. David Walker, for instance, was a regular guest at Burlingham House and Tristan Ballance, John Wood and the Rought-Roughts all moved easily in their skipper's social circles. Nor did being a professional rule a player out from the benefits of Michael Falcon's pastoral care, as his role in the development of Bill Edrich' s career showed; he went out of his way to ensure that Bill achieved his ambition to play first-class county cricket, even though Bill's departure was a great loss to Norfolk cricket. After the Second World War, Falcon was similarly active in introducing Bill's brothers, Geoff and Eric, to the first-class game.

1930

Norfolk had a poor year in 1930 due to a severe breakdown in the batting. Of the regulars, only Falcon and John Coldham averaged over 20 and the former was most inconsistent. In the season's opener against Surrey II he became one of the first batsmen to have an innings described as 'Bradmanesque', hitting up 120 with three sixes and 18 fours. As usual with a big Falcon innings, his driving on both sides of the wicket was powerful, but he also deployed shots all round the rest of the ground. In the second match, against Kent II, he hit 28 and 72 not out so that his average stood at an impressive 110. Inexplicably he then lost all form, scoring 69 runs in his next ten innings, at which point the *Eastern Daily Press* tersely announced that he would be unavailable for the two games against Lincolnshire as he was going to Scotland. With the ball Falcon was similarly inconsistent, taking six for 24 and four for 60 in losing causes against Buckinghamshire, but no more than 13 wickets in all. Again, he was the most costly of the regular bowlers as age was beginning to tell. As the local daily commented: 'The four overs Michael Falcon bowled at The Oval after his fine display of hitting were not sent down at the fast pace formerly associated with the Norfolk captain and he had only one slip.' In his six-wicket return against Buckinghamshire his pace was merely 'medium-fast' and he relied on keeping an excellent length for his wickets.

1931

Michael Falcon had a poor season with the bat, averaging less than 20 with a hard-hit 47 against Surrey II being his best. He did, however, put in a good all-round performance against Kent II enabling Norfolk to win in the only day on which play was possible: he took two for 20 and six for 39 and made 30 and 17 not out as Norfolk won by nine wickets with five minutes to spare. The *Eastern Daily Press* commented: 'Falcon bowled ... faster than is now expected of him. He put every ounce of energy into his work, and played a big part in the brilliant victory of his side ... he is by no means a spent force as a bowler.' As it turned out, he took only another 11 wickets all season and this was the penultimate five-wicket haul of his Norfolk career.

When the New Zealanders visited Norwich to play Norfolk, Falcon arranged to entertain them by laying on a visit to the Theatre Royal, where there was a performance of E.W.Hornung's *Raffles* by the Norwich Repertory Company. About ten of the tourists accompanied their host to the production.

1932

Norfolk had another poor year with the bat and Falcon's form again petered out after a good start: he made 56 and 64 not out as Lincolnshire were routed in a fixture made notable by Jack Lingwood's sixteen-wicket return.[49] No more fifties came his way but, in the last match of the season, he played a 'courageous captain's innings' combining well with the sixteen-year-old Bill Edrich, who made his maiden Championship fifty, to delay an innings defeat by Buckinghamshire. His bowling at Minor County level was not well-rewarded, but he had one remarkable success in a club game. Turning out for Great Yarmouth he was almost single-handedly responsible for dismissing his old side, Norwich Wanderers, for 50, conceding only six runs in taking eight wickets.

---

49   His match figures of 16 for 74 are the second best for Norfolk in the Minor Counties Championship, behind only the 16 for 72 returned by slow left-armer Charlie Shore against Durham in 1897.

*Michael Falcon, apparently ready to bowl, leads out the Norfolk side against
Buckinghamshire in August 1931.
In view, from l to r, J.C.Thistleton-Smith, J.M.Coldham, Michael Falcon,
D.F.Walker, G.N.Scott-Chad, N.L.Foster, B.W.Rought-Rought, W.G.Eagle,
D.C.Rought-Rought.*

*Players and officials in the Norfolk v 'All-India' match at Lakenham in June 1932.
Standing (l to r): J.E.Nichols (umpire), Jahangir Khan, E.C.W.Ricketts (All-India
manager), Mohammad Nissar, J.C.Thistleton-Smith, P.E.Palia, N.L.Foster, Amar
Singh, W.J.Lingwood, B.E.Kapadia, H.E.Theobald, S.Nazir Ali, G.J.Rye
(umpire).
Seated: S.H.M.Colah, A.G.Utting, S.Wazir Ali, B.W.Rought-Rought,
K.S.Ganshyamsinhji of Limbdi, M.Falcon, Joginder Singh, G.N.Scott-Chad,
C.K.Nayudu, D.C.Rought-Rought.
On the ground: N.D.Marshall, A.W.Tyler, Naoomal Jeoomal, Ghulam
Mohammad, W.J.Edrich.
This was Edrich's first match for the county.*

1933

This was a great year for Norfolk who won four games outright and led on the first innings in five of the other six fixtures. They finished top of the Championship table and were duly challenged by Yorkshire II. Playing at Lakenham, Norfolk performed poorly, being dismissed for 147 and 122 and losing by nine wickets. Their nemesis was the spin-bowling of James Heaton who took 11 wickets, with no fewer than six falling to stumpings by Syd Buller. Michael Falcon led the resistance in the first innings, playing an innings which 'was a typical effort of a courageous captain ... fine and forcing.' As is well known, when the final table was being checked in November 1933 for insertion in *Wisden*, it was found that its columns did not agree. The percentages were recalculated and it was found that Wiltshire, with 70.00 and previously thought to be third and not Yorkshire II, with 68.33, had in fact finished in second place. (Norfolk's percentage was 72.00, incidentally.) The play-off was entirely spurious, as 'Yorkshire had no standing in the matter'. It was too late to organize a second play-off and the title was officially left 'not decided', rather as it had been in 1912, Falcon's first year as skipper.[50]

Falcon played a typical bits-and-pieces role in Norfolk's success: although his highest score (70) was almost inevitably in his first match, the falling-off in his batting was not as marked as in the previous couple of years. He also collected 12 wickets spread throughout the season. An example of his team-spirit was to be found in the game against Kent II in which, due to a breakdown in

---

50   Writing in *The Cricketer Annual* of 1933/34, the MCCA secretary, R.C. Campbell, said that the problem was caused by 'insufficient information on the official score sheet from Yorkshire as to the actual result' of the match between Yorkshire II and Staffordshire at Sheffield on 12 and 13 July. Since Norfolk had no involvement in any of this, the frustration to the county's players must have been very great. Understandably, the Yorkshire hierarchy was distinctly unhappy. For example, Sir Stanley Jackson stated that: 'The matter will have to be referred to the MCC for their decision as to whether the Yorkshire team are the Minor Counties Champions or not.' (Perhaps he thought that the presence of himself and Lord Hawke on the MCC Committee was likely to lead to a favourable outcome for his county.) Surprisingly, the Norfolk administration did not seem to be at all perturbed by the whole *débâcle*. Desmond Buxton, the Norfolk secretary, declared, 'I am more amused than cross at the affair', and, when asked if Norfolk would play a challenge match against Wiltshire in early 1934, he made the valid point that many of the amateurs might not be available but concluded that 'if it were done it would be rather fun'. Nor did Norfolk's supporters overwhelm the local press with indignant complaints; no letters of outrage found their way to the correspondence columns of the *Eastern Daily Press*. Elsewhere in this book, Bill Edrich will be quoted on how hard the Norfolk team had tried to win the Championship; given their efforts, quite what they made of the lack of support from their administrators can only be imagined.

communication whilst running between the wickets, Falcon and David Walker found themselves at the same end. The skipper, knowing full well who was the better batsman, sacrificed his wicket without a second thought.

1934

Speaking at the annual dinner of the Norwich Wanderers club, Michael Falcon spoke of an alteration to the lbw law which was being considered by the MCC Committee, and of which he was in favour, but he feared that the Minor Counties Championship might be used as a testing ground for experimentation, as had happened once before, in 1902.[51] He also urged for an improvement in the standard of local wickets.

Following their triumphant season in 1933, Norfolk had another good campaign in the following year. Going into the final match against Cambridgeshire, they needed to win the match outright to secure a place in the Challenge Match. Cambridgeshire were made to follow-on but they batted through most of the second day and secured a draw. Michael Falcon had a poor year: after commencing with a 54, he scored few runs in the rest of the year and averaged less than 20. With the ball there was no longer any pretence at pace as his slows captured a mere four expensive wickets. Over his entire career this was one of the few years in which he least merited his place in the team as a player; his captaincy was still up to scratch though as the *Eastern Daily Press* reported: 'Falcon managed the bowling with the alert and keen observing mind of the experienced captain' and again 'his long experience was a valuable asset in his admirable leadership.'

1935

In March Geoffrey Colman died. Educated at Eton and Oxford (where he would have been captain of cricket in 1915 if the Great War had not intervened), he was severely wounded during the War

---

51 As is well known, an experiment was indeed made with the lbw Law in 1935, but it was conducted in the first-class game as well as in Minor Counties fixtures. Whereas previously the ball had to pitch in a straight line between the wickets in order to be a candidate for a successful lbw appeal, it was now allowed to pitch on the off-side of the wicket, providing it hit the batsman in a line between the wickets and (obviously) was going on to hit the stumps. Decisions made under the new ruling were to be 'Noted with the sign '(N)' in the scorebook.' The experiment was considered to be a success and was formally incorporated into the Laws on 5 May 1937.

and was able to play for Norfolk only intermittently thereafter. He was great friends with Michael Falcon who attended the funeral and later delivered a eulogy to Colman at the Norfolk club's annual meeting.

Norfolk continued to shine in 1935, winning five games outright and conceding first innings leads only to arch-rivals Buckinghamshire. The batting was very much a team effort with seven players averaging over 26. Michael Falcon demonstrated much improved form, amassing 397 runs at an average of 30.54. He played aggressively all season and was only overshone in the away fixture with Buckinghamshire. The last man Wilfrid Thompson came in to join him when Norfolk, who had followed on, were a mere 31 ahead. Thompson proceeded to pummel 58 out of a partnership of 67 in 25 minutes: he hit four sixes, breaking a cottage window, then losing two balls and finishing off by smashing the window of a car parked near the pavilion. By then Norfolk were safe. Falcon took a mere nine wickets all season but did have one match-winning spell: in the first game of the season Hertfordshire were made to follow on and Falcon's four for 44 in the second innings was instrumental in setting up Norfolk's ten wicket victory with a mere ten minutes to spare. His captaincy continued to receive favourable notice in the *Eastern Daily Press*: 'the captain ... making the best possible use of the bowling at his command'.

1936

Norfolk's unbeaten run in the Championship continued into 1936 when, with three outright wins, they finished second to Hertfordshire. As they had played Hertfordshire in the regular season, they were unable to issue a challenge for the title: this was frustrating as Norfolk had had very much the better of Hertfordshire in the two fixtures between the counties. They won the first by ten wickets and, in the second, Hertfordshire, following on, were a mere six runs ahead with three wickets remaining when time ran out. Slow left-armer Tristan Ballance was largely responsible for this dominance, his hauls against Hertfordshire totalling 21 wickets for 113 runs. These feats helped him to a highly impressive total of 42 wickets at 8.11 apiece. The other bowlers had supporting roles with, surprisingly, Michael Falcon returning the most economical figures: he took 17 wickets at less than 12, chipping in almost every time he had a bowl. His deadliest spell was three for 5 as he sent back the Lincolnshire middle order. With the bat, Michael Falcon contributed little, other than a 65 against Kent II.

Remarkably, there was crowd unrest at Lakenham, where the home crowd took against Walter Franklin. To quote the *Eastern Daily Press*: 'The frequency with which he felt justified in appealing on Monday afternoon kept the umpires alert and some of the bobsiders registered their disapproval.' Michael Falcon's view of Franklin, characteristically mild and diplomatic, was that 'he talked too much'. On this occasion, though, his verbosity encouraged the umpires into giving Buckinghamshire six lbw decisions out of the total of nine Norfolk wickets which fell.

1937

In February Michael Falcon was elected to chair the Yarmouth and Gorleston Conservative Association, thereby resuming political activity (albeit behind the scenes) after a gap of fourteen years. He was to pilot the local party through the tricky years of a wartime alliance between the Conservatives and the Liberals that was reminiscent of the coalition that he was part of as an MP in the 1918 election.

In 1937 Norfolk increased their fixture list to twelve matches, with Middlesex II as new opponents, perhaps a reflection of their captain's influence at Lord's. They lost Championship games for the first time since 1932 and slipped to tenth in the table. Both batting and bowling averages looked strong on paper so the final position in the table was a little disappointing. Michael Falcon had another good 'bits-and-pieces' year: he topped 450 runs with four fifties and took 20 reasonably cheap wickets with a haul of five for 49 against Cambridgeshire at Hunstanton proving to be the final five-wicket analysis of his Minor County career. The wicket was conducive to spin and he exploited it cleverly. Against Hertfordshire at Cokenach, Falcon helped Eric Edrich to put on 171 for the fifth wicket, still a record for Norfolk. He was very much the junior partner in the stand, scoring only 69, but he was still making runs all round the wicket. Despite the lengthened Minor Counties season, Falcon had plenty of time for social cricket, the most important match being between Overstrand, captained by Falcon, and Sir Julien Cahn's XI which was staged to raise funds to help save Overstrand's ground from development. The game, which was ruined by rain, was one of many fund-raisers in which Falcon turned out for the benefit of cricket facilities in Norfolk: he was always very enthusiastic about improving the sporting 'infrastructure' in his native county.

1938

Michael Falcon won the toss for Norfolk eleven times out of twelve in this season. His batting was less consistent and rather more typical of his later years; an opening full of promise followed by a loss of form. After three matches he had scored 162 runs for just three dismissals, a 54 against Hertfordshire getting something of a rave review in the *Eastern Daily Press*: 'Falcon exploited all his strokes, making lovely leg glances, some superb and powerful drives, and several fine hooks.' Subsequently he scored so poorly that his final average was below 20. His bowling figures also looked poor – only ten wickets at 25.20. However, they hide a couple of match-winning performances. Against Kent II at Gravesend, when the rest of the attack laboured to dismiss Kent for the second time, he nipped in with a spell of three for 20 to set up a five-wicket victory with minutes to spare. Even more impressively, against Cambridgeshire, he bowled extremely well to take four for 34: 'from a good length he was always moving the ball, coming swiftly off the pitch, and frequently beating the bat.' His partnership with Tristan Ballance, who took the other six wickets, constituted a match-winning attack on this occasion.

In friendly cricket Michael Falcon continued to turn out for a variety of teams (East Norfolk, Church of England's Young Men's Society, Norfolk Club and Ground, Norwich Union) but the highlight of the social season was expected to be the All-Edrich match. Set for the 14 September, a match between Michael Falcon's Norfolk and an All-Edrich Eleven starring Bill, the newly capped Test player, was proposed by the local rector to raise funds for a new recreation ground at Blofield. The BBC 'wireless' men were to be present and there was a fair crowd gathered, despite steady drizzle. In an early example of sport dancing to a broadcaster's tune, Michael Falcon's team batted first and knocked up a rapid 132 for two before declaring to give Bill a chance to take first knock for his family team and be at the wicket in time for the radio broadcast. The new ball was given to George Pilch, who came from the same family as Fuller Pilch,[52] but not thought likely to pose many problems for a Test star. He ran up and delivered his first ball which Bill, to everybody's horror, glided straight into the hands of Rodney Rought-Rought, at first slip, who didn't think quickly enough to drop the ball. Bill returned to the pavilion to general consternation, his part in the game over before the BBC had swung into action. Shortly afterwards rain caused the abandonment of the game. Rev A Shilleto had sold £70 of tickets before the day and, despite the weather, over £100 was raised in total. Bill's grandfather made a speech 'expressing his pride in his children and grandchildren and his appreciation of Mr Michael Falcon's readiness to assist in the upkeep of the Recreation Ground.' This wasn't the only testimonial paid to Falcon in 1938, the year of his fiftieth birthday. He received a telegram: 'All members of Norfolk County Cricket Club send you heartiest congratulations on your fiftieth birthday, and their deepest gratitude for all your magnificent services to Norfolk cricket, which they hope may be long continued.' The *Eastern Daily Press* added to the general approval of the county captain: 'Mention should be made of Michael Falcon's skilful captaincy and especially of the way in which he managed to get the best out of the somewhat limited bowling at his disposal.'

1939

Norfolk finished in mid-table again in the final pre-war season made notable by David Walker and Harold Theobald setting a new record for a Minor Counties Championship first-wicket partnership. They put on 323 against Northumberland, largely due to Walker who scored 217.[53] The batting of Michael Falcon was also remarkable; in an Indian summer of strokeplay, Falcon passed fifty on no fewer than six times, a feat he had achieved in only two seasons before. Although he made no score of more than 79, he racked up 552 runs, quite an achievement for a 'veteran'. His batting once more earned good reviews all season, consisting of 'skilful leg glances and clean leg hitting and driving'. The press

---

52   Although later Pilches who played for Norfolk (R.G., G.E. and D.G.) are sometimes described as direct descendants of Fuller Pilch, they are not, for Fuller Pilch died childless.

53   This remained a record for this wicket in the Minor Counties Championship until Carl Rogers and Carl Amos, also of Norfolk, put on 335 against Hertfordshire at Hertford in 2002.

commented that 'An outstanding feature of the Norfolk season has been the consistently sound and often brilliant batting of the captain. Several times his was the highest score in an innings and many times Michael Falcon went in after those before him had done poorly and when a critical stage had been reached.' A highlight was his innings of 42 against the West Indians which helped Norfolk to a first-innings lead in a drawn game. His success surpassed even his form of 1937; quite why he should have had such triumphs after a few relatively fallow years and at such an advanced age is a mystery. It allows us, though, to say of Michael Falcon that his batting career was significantly interrupted by both World Wars, which puts him in a very small club indeed.

Possibly the only action photograph of Michael Falcon batting. Taken in 1939.

Life At North Burlingham: 1931-1969

After several years at Havering-atte-Bower, Essex, making his living as a merchant of hops, Michael Falcon decided on a career change. In 1930 his father introduced him to the Norwich Union Insurance Society and he became a non-executive director of the company in 1936. (His father had been President from 1930 to 1936.) The following year he bought into the brewing firm of Lacon's, a sizeable concern founded in the eighteenth century, its shares quoted on the London Stock Exchange, with its main brewery[54] in Great Yarmouth and over 300 'tied' houses. The only son of the chairman, Ernest Lacon, had died young – he also had three daughters – and Michael Falcon was to act almost as a surrogate 'son' until the old man's grandsons were old enough to join him on the board. In the event Ernest Lacon died in June 1936, so that Falcon became the company's deputy chairman and later chairman, in charge of the day-to-day running of the business for

---

54   The Lacon company trademark was a falcon, but this predated the Falcon family's involvement with the business and seems to have been an odd coincidence.

many years.[55] He also joined the board of Great Yarmouth Water Works.

*The former Lacon brewery warehouse in Great Yarmouth,
showing the company's falcon trade mark.
The site is now partly occupied by a casino.*

These new jobs allowed him to sell up in Essex and return to live in his beloved Norfolk – which was probably their main attraction. In 1931 Falcon rented Burlingham House, a sizeable property, built in 1790, in North Burlingham, a village midway between Norwich and Great Yarmouth, from Frank Price, a local man in the retailing business. He subsequently bought the property which was to become his home for the next thirty-eight years. Whilst residence in Essex had not prevented him from turning out for Norfolk as a player any more than being an MP had, he had been unable to play much of a role in the administration of cricket in his home county whilst living so far away. His move to Burlingham House gave him the opportunity to rejoin the likes of C.B.L.Prior and R.G.Pilch in looking after the management of Norfolk cricket and to participate

---

55   Not surprisingly, first-class cricketers have had something of a predilection for brewery directorships. Between the wars, about twenty such players were brewery directors, including Frank Mann, Falcon's former Cambridge colleague, referred to earlier in this tale. The Lacon board during Falcon's time included C.E.Lucas, who had played occasionally for Cambridge University and Sussex between 1906 and 1908.

The Falcon family lived here, at Burlingham House, North Burlingham, from 1931 to 1969.

in the training of young cricketers such as Bill Edrich. There was another advantage that life in North Burlingham had over Essex: it provided an excellent place in which someone who was a countryman at heart could raise his family.

Falcon had one son, Michael Gascoigne Falcon, and four daughters, Mary, Sybil, Anne and Rachel. Unfortunately Mary, who was born in 1921 and whose godfather was family friend and England Test captain Frank Mann, suffered from Down's Syndrome and died in 1948. Michael Gascoigne, and Sybil Edwards, who spent most of their childhood at Burlingham, retain happy memories of their upbringing and of their father's life in rural Norfolk. His day would invariably start with a spell of bowling in his own home-made net – there had also been a net at his father's home at Horstead House – followed by a run around the field in front of the house. He would don a pair of shorts for this run, which was not cancelled even for rain: in the event of damp weather there was a hat kept specifically for the purpose. Up until 1939 a cold bath followed, but this was replaced by a wash in a hip-bath under the pump near the kitchen-garden. Apparently he could be heard by the neighbouring farmer on the other side of the wall 'a-shuddering'. Breakfast was relatively spartan, consisting of a bowl of porridge (with salt rather than sugar) which he would make himself and, when they were available, an orange. He had developed a taste for oranges when he was serving in Palestine during the Great War and was bivouacked in citrus orchards along with the horses in his care.

Michael Falcon enjoyed returning to the county of his father's birth and walking across the fells of Cumberland, but he had two major hobbies at Burlingham House which gave him great pleasure. One involved the preparation and care of turf for cricket pitches and lawn tennis courts. He was a great believer in the use of soil collected from the nearby Acle marshes. He constructed two tennis courts at Burlingham, which were his pride and joy. Sybil Edwards remembers that these courts had superb surfaces and were a scene of much enjoyment for family and friends alike. Michael Falcon spent hours weeding his courts, removing daisies, moss, plantains and clover. He also 'exported' his expertise, being responsible for the preparation of cricket pitches at places such as Britannia Barracks, close to Norwich Prison, on a hill overlooking the city. His other hobby was the cultivation of fruit trees: he took great care in selecting the varieties of fruit that he grew so that the apple, pear and peach seasons were unusually long. He was enormously proud of his harvest which was a source of great enjoyment, especially when rationing reared its ugly head.[56]

Michael and Kathleen Falcon at Loweswater, Cumberland in 1937.

In the garden at North Burlingham in 1933; note the Norfolk jacket.

---

56   Whilst Falcon was tending his fruit trees at Burlingham House, just down the road was an organisation called the Burlingham Demonstration Station whose purpose was the development of new varieties of fruit. This seems to have been a coincidence and Michael Falcon had little direct contact with it.

Michael Gascoigne Falcon remembers that his father was very keen that he should continue to uphold the family name in the cricket world. In order to give his son an early advantage over other boys, Falcon had constructed a special net with a built-in slope which exactly replicated the famous slope at Lord's. In this way he hoped his son would be properly prepared to cope with one of the major hazards of big cricket, a problem which was well known to perplex even experienced cricketers who were playing on it for the first time. He also made a yearly telephone call to his son's headmaster in which he would nervously enquire as to how his son was progressing as a cricketer. Unfortunately for Michael Falcon, his son had inherited absolutely none of his father's ability and, whilst this caused him disappointment, he was too good a father to let this adversely affect his relationship with his son who remembers the whole episode with wry amusement. (His name only appears once in the *Eastern Daily Press* cricket columns; in a colts match in which he failed to trouble the scorers. Whilst doing National Service he boxed a little but was not a natural sportsman.) It was his sister, Sybil Edwards, who inherited her father's sporting enthusiasm and ability: she was a regular attender at Lakenham as a teenager and when she went up to Cambridge to read geography (being resident at Newnham College between 1944 and 1947) she won blues at both cricket and lacrosse. She was captain of the University eleven in 1946 and remembers that her father taught her to be a slow bowler and 'was a huge support and encouragement', taking great delight in her successes.[57]

Before the Second World War, Michael Falcon would take his young children to visit their grandparents, who had moved to Sprowston Hall, for tea every Sunday. (Michael Falcon senior lived to the age of 80, passing on in April 1939. The funeral was held at Horstead Church, followed by a service at Sprowston Hall which was attended by the widow and all four children.) Then, when they went away to boarding schools and universities, he would

---

[57] There is an uncanny resemblance to my own family here. My father was a good club cricketer, nowhere near Falcon's standard but good enough to share the new-ball with John Price in Forces cricket in Germany and was desperately keen for me to follow in his footsteps. Unfortunately, like Falcon's son, I was hopeless and it was my sister who went on to win Blues at cricket and lacrosse like Sybil, at Oxford rather than Cambridge. Where the story diverges is that, although I was inept I was exceedingly keen and continued to play doggedly at a low level in Norfolk. Eventually age caught up with my father and he quit 'decent' cricket before retiring back to Norfolk: at this point I invited him to resume his career by playing alongside me. We appeared together for a couple of years, which was most enjoyable, and in the end I was the one who first called it a day.

devotedly write to each on a Sunday, carrying the letters by foot to the postbox on North Burlingham Green regardless of the weather. Given a good start in life by caring parents – not forgetting the role played by their mother – Falcon's children did well for themselves. Sybil's junior twin sister Anne went to the Slade School of Art and became an artist, marrying Peter Arkell, who came from a family of brewers. Their younger sister Rachel studied history at St. Hilda's College, Oxford and married John Clark. Michael Gascoigne followed his father into the brewery business, becoming head brewer and later joint managing director of E.Lacon and Co Ltd, which was taken over by Whitbread in 1965, and also onto the board of Norwich Union, a position in which he was by no means overshadowed by either his father or his grandfather. As well as his activities in brewing and insurance he was chairman of the National Seed Development Organisation from 1972 until 1982, being appointed CBE in 1979 'for services to the seed industry'. He was also much involved with St. John Ambulance and has been the High Steward of Great Yarmouth for the past 25 years. In 2009 he was awarded the honorary freedom of the borough of Great Yarmouth.[58] Of all the children, Sybil had perhaps the most interesting life, dedicating herself to missionary work in South Africa and allowing herself only infrequent trips back to England. When she finished her labours abroad she returned home to look after her widowed mother and later married the Very Rev David Edwards, who had been Dean of Norwich and then Provost of Southwark.

Finishing this brief look at the Falcon family it would doubtless have pleased the old cricketer to know that he has several young male descendants who are, according to his son, capable and enthusiastic cricketers. Perhaps the name of Falcon will reappear in first-class or Norfolk cricket?

When Falcon and his wife left Burlingham House in 1969 they sold it to the local society for mentally handicapped people who converted it into a permanent residence for adults with learning disabilities. When the facilities were extended into the stable

---

58   Indeed two acquaintances of mine who have worked for Norwich Union thought, when told that I was writing a biography of Michael Falcon but not told that cricket was involved, that the book would be about Michael Gascoigne Falcon rather than his father. He married April Lambert and had three children; Claire, Michael and Andrew – the last of whom chaired the Eastern Region of the Royal Forestry Society. After Whitbread closed down the Lacon brewery in 1968, he joined the board of another East Anglian brewer, Greene King and chaired local health authorities.

block, a development which was largely funded by a donation from Kathleen Falcon, it was named Mary Falcon House in memory of the Falcons' late daughter. Michael Gascoigne Falcon was involved in the running of the facility as a member of the management committee until 2009 when the home was finally closed and the 28 people then in residence were rehoused.

Bill Edrich

Now that Bill Edrich has stepped into the story, this may be an appropriate point to recount some of the details of his early association with Michael Falcon.

It was in the early thirties that Bill Edrich burst upon the Norfolk cricket scene with his performances for Bracondale School, a small private school located in Norwich which has since closed down. Michael Falcon and county coach, Jack Nichols, took note and arranged that young Bill, at 15 young enough to qualify for the Junior Colts, should turn out for the Senior Colts instead in the annual trial match. He duly made runs and took wickets. Falcon, who was captain of Norfolk's premier club, Norwich Wanderers, offered Bill a few games. Bill was eternally grateful for the encouragement and the coaching he received from the county captain as will be described below in Chapter Ten and was rewarded for some fine performances by being selected to make his debut for Norfolk in early June 1932 as a 16-year-old schoolboy against All India. The Indians batted first and were shot out for just 101 as Norfolk's bowlers excelled themselves, but then Norfolk went down before the pace attack of Mohammad Nissar, reaching just 49, of which Bill Edrich top-scored with a highly creditable 20. Following this success, Bill was drafted into Norfolk's Minor Counties Championship side but he made an inauspicious start against Leicestershire II: he was clean bowled in both innings without scoring and collected a 'pair'. Michael Falcon kept faith with the youngster through a lean spell until, in the last match of the season, against the Championship winners Buckinghamshire, Bill top-scored in both innings with 50 and 23. A batting average of 15 barely hinted at what was to come for Edrich.

Bill improved rapidly in the next couple of seasons, receiving his county colours at the age of just 17. He was part of the side which pushed so hard for the Minor Counties Championship in 1933. Edrich recounted how Michael Falcon, deprived by the flooding in the autumn of 1912 of leading his county to the title in his inaugural season as captain, was keen to capture the Championship and how his team were right behind him: 'In the team we had made up our minds that our popular captain should have his triumph if human flesh and blood could achieve it.' How administrative error prevented Norfolk from claiming the title has been described above. Bill remembered how, meanwhile, Falcon guided him in the ways of cricket, described in Compton and Edrich's *Cricket and All That*:

> 'What field?' he would ask as I paced out my run-up in early matches for Norfolk. 'Three slips, gully, cover, forward short leg, deep fine leg ... ' ' He would halt me abruptly. 'Are you bowling on the leg stump?' 'No, off stump, sir.' I would stammer. 'Then you won't be needing a deep fine leg, William', he would say kindly. I soon learned to pitch a good line.

Bill continued to flourish under Falcon's wise leadership, but, even before taking a fine century off the 1935 South Africans, he was making plans to become a first-class county cricketer. Like his county captain twenty years before him, Bill was born in Norfolk and so would have to qualify for a first-class county by residing within its boundaries for two years before he could turn out in the County Championship. The sources on how Bill ended up qualifying for Middlesex are not consistent but a certain pattern emerges. According to Sir Home Gordon, the initiative lay with Michael Falcon, who told young Edrich that he was too good for the Minor County Championship and contacted Kent on Bill's behalf. Kent turned Falcon down, saying that they had nowhere to place Bill in the winters whilst he was qualifying. Not disheartened, Falcon tried Middlesex who were more receptive and agreed to take Bill onto the groundstaff. According to Ralph Barker, author of *The Cricketing Family Edrich*, Alan Hill, author of *Bill Edrich: A Biography* and, perhaps most persuasively, Bill's autobiography, *Cricket Heritage*, the initial move was made by Bill himself. He wrote to Northamptonshire, the nearest and the poorest of the first-class counties, asking for a trial. Either Bill, on receiving a response that could be called non-committal, turned to Michael Falcon for advice or the county captain heard of Bill's letter and went to the Edrich family house in Lingwood to offer his opinion. Falcon was at first reluctant to push Bill forward, knowing that the professional game was a gamble, but was soon persuaded by Bill's evident keenness to help the youngster. According to Bill's autobiography, the approach to Kent happened then and was followed by the successful application to Middlesex. Barker and Hill, on the other hand, have Falcon, with obvious ambition that Bill should play for England, going straight for Middlesex, declaring that 'cricketers were apt to go unnoticed in the provinces. They should play at Headquarters, where the scribes were, and where they were continually under the eye of the people who mattered.'

The next time Michael Falcon went to Lord's for an MCC committee meeting he had a word with the Club's secretary, Billy Findlay, saying that Middlesex would soon be needing young batsmen to take over from the likes of the ageing Patsy Hendren and 'Young' Jack Hearne and that Bill Edrich was just the sort of cricketer for them. Hence Bill was sent for a trial in April 1934 – despite severely mangling his right hand in a farm accident shortly before his big day – he did well enough to be accepted onto the MCC 'second-class' groundstaff with permission to continue to play for Norfolk during his qualification period.

Bill Edrich's exploits in first-class and Test cricket are well-known and need no re-telling here. What is less well-known to those outside Norfolk is that he returned to captain his native county once his first-class career was over, proving to be a daring, innovative captain who drew the crowds back to Lakenham after a fallow period in the 1950s. David Armstrong is the best source on the strengths of Edrich as a skipper, but Ralph Barker also had a point to make, suggesting that Bill's leadership was so radical (for example, sacrificing first-innings points in the search for outright wins) that some old timers such as Michael Falcon took a while to adjust and that they were eventually won over only by the succession of exciting finishes brought about by Bill's challenging declarations. In truth Bill was merely ahead of his time, as the two-day Minor Counties match eventually went the same way as the three-day first-class county match. On ever-improving wickets both were found to be unfinishable without declarations and artificial run-chases on the final afternoon, and both have been consigned to history to the benefit of players and spectators alike.[59] Whatever, Bill Edrich repaid his 'debt' to Michael Falcon by coming back to Norfolk.

---

59   As an interesting aside, the first suggestion that I can trace that two days was insufficient for a Minor Counties match was made by an ex-skipper of Norfolk, Brereton Knyvet Wilson, as early as 1937.

Chapter Seven
Second World War and Beyond

Now aged 51, Michael Falcon was too old for active service, but the majority of his Norfolk team-mates were eligible and were duly called up. The process started whilst the 1939 cricket season was still in mid-flow: Basil Rought-Rought and John Wood found themselves with the 5th Norfolks in Sussex as early as 17 July, although, as Basil managed to get leave for a few games, that was little hardship. In contrast to the situation in 1914 at the start of First World War, the 1939 season was finished before hostilities broke out and, although preparations for war were taking place at the same time as the cricket, no Norfolk matches were cancelled and few players were rendered unavailable due to the call of duty. Michael Falcon did his best for Geoff Edrich, who had been offered a professional engagement with Hampshire for 1940, by getting his call-up for the militia deferred until the end of the 1939 season, in the hope that the world situation would improve, but of course it was a vain wish. By the time Geoff had to report to Colchester to sign up, all hope of playing for Hampshire in 1940 had vanished.

Michael Falcon did his bit by signing up for the Local Defence Volunteers, later to be renamed the Home Guard, and was appointed commander of the 14th Platoon, 4th Company, 6th Battalion of the Norfolk Home Guard, based at Lingwood. His son, Michael Gascoigne, remembers that Falcon brought the same thorough, competitive nature to civil defence as he did to Minor Counties cricket. Exercises were often carried out at Holkham Hall and Thetford Heath and Falcon's platoon were regular winners of trophies such as the battalion and divisional championships for tactical battle drill. His daughter, Sybil, remembers that her father was immensely proud of his platoon, which was made up of local farming men who, she said, would have followed him anywhere. His gift of leadership was not confined to the cricket field. Sybil's sister, Anne, recalls that Falcon's Sunday mornings during the war were taken up with Home Guard duties, which he would conduct with immense enthusiasm and dedication, dressed in thick khaki and with huge regulation boots. He would return to Burlingham

House in time to preside over Sunday luncheon, but rarely in time to change so that he would eat in uniform and change into civvies after the meal.

Between 1940 and 1944, Michael Falcon commanded this platoon of the Home Guard based in Lingwood.

Little cricket of significance was played in Norfolk during the Second World War, but there were plenty of other duties besides the Home Guard to keep Michael Falcon busy. His directorship of Lacon's Brewery continued, as did his work for the Norwich Union, where speaking at packed Annual Meetings was part and parcel of the job. He remained a magistrate, operating in the east of Norfolk, and was honoured in 1943 by being appointed High Sheriff of Norfolk, an office which his father had held before him.

It being wartime, his list of ceremonial duties was probably lighter than was normal for the holder of the office of High Sheriff. In contrast, his political activities kept him busy throughout the war. In 1941, Great Yarmouth's sitting

Michael Falcon, in court dress as High Sheriff of Norfolk, in 1943.

MP, Sir Arthur Harbord, died. As chairman of the Yarmouth and Gorleston Co-ordinating Committee, Michael Falcon was responsible for overseeing the selection of the Liberal, Mr Percy Jewson (a former Lord Major of Norwich), as the National Government candidate. Jewson was duly elected, unopposed. Nor was that the end of his many duties: in February 1943, for example, six Canadian soldiers were welcomed to lunch by the Lord Mayor of Great Yarmouth, following which they were given a guided tour of the town, seeing bomb damage and places of interest, conducted by Falcon acting in his role as chairman of the local Ministry of Information committee.

Meanwhile, as Michael Falcon was busying himself with his various administrative duties, the war went on and casualties amongst the Norfolk players inevitably occurred. The first draftees, Basil Rought-Rought and John Wood, were reported as missing in action as early as 20 July 1940 and news of Geoff Edrich's imprisonment by the Japanese whilst serving in the Far East was similarly described. In the end the only fatalities suffered amongst the regular Norfolk squad of the late 1930s were David Walker, who was killed whilst flying over Norway in February 1942 and buried in Trondheim, and Tristan Ballance, who was killed near Naples in December 1943. Michael Falcon, who was particularly close to David Walker, took these losses hard.[60]

In November 1944, Michael Falcon's duties with the Home Guard came to an end as the 6th Battalion of the Norfolk Home Guard had a 'stand down' parade at Britannia Barracks, receiving official thanks from Field Marshal Lord Ironside and a farewell from their commanding officer, Colonel A.R.Taylor. Falcon's daughter Anne recalls that, when released from their military duties, many of the men in her father's platoon reunited to form the Burlingham Bowling Club which played its matches on summer evenings on the lawn in front of Burlingham House. (Although she does not say, the chances are that Falcon himself would have tended the lawn!) In time the club acquired their own hut on the green at North Burlingham.

As civil defence duties were wound down, cricketing matters recommenced and the Norfolk C.C.C. committee made

---

60   Other Norfolk players who lost their lives in the Second World War were John Bally (whose cricketing heyday was in the twenties), David Colman (son of Geoffrey Colman), James Jackson, Alexander Barton, Gordon Thorne and Alan Colman.

preparations for restarting county cricket – the club had closed down during the war with no subscriptions being taken. The following letter, signed by Michael Falcon, C.B.L.Prior and J.W.Corran – respectively captain, chairman and acting secretary of the club – appeared in the *Eastern Daily Press*, dated 21 May 1945:

> Although the war with Germany is over, it is not expected that Norfolk C.C.C. will be in a position to participate in matches this season, as many of its potential players are still in the services. In spite of this we desire to make a start this season by arranging Norfolk Club and Ground matches. The main object of [these] is to enable the county selectors to keep in touch with young cricketers from schools and clubs. In order to enable this object to be attained any cricketers who would like to be considered for selection to represent the Club and Ground are invited to send their names and addresses to the Acting Honorary Secretary ... as soon as possible. In doing so they should say whether they are batsmen or bowlers and give some details of their previous clubs. The co-operation of all cricketers and cricket clubs is requested in these first efforts to restart cricket in the county.

As well as seeking new blood on the field, the County committee also launched a membership drive, as was reported in a 'Circular Letter to Members and Prospective Members' issued in February 1946 above the names of C.B.L.Prior (now chairman), M.Falcon (still captain) and D.G.Buxton (the new secretary). This also reported that the Lakenham ground was in need of considerable renovation; that C.S.R.Boswell had been re-engaged as a professional for a further year; and that six county fixtures had been arranged for the 1946 season.

The Club and Ground matches in 1945 were considered a success, but no new players were discovered who were both mature and talented enough to make a significant impact as soon as 1946, when it was decided that the Championship would recommence. Thus things looked fairly bleak for Norfolk. As well as losing Walker and Ballance, the following players from the squad of the late 1930s were also no longer available to the county: Rodney Rought-Rought (one of Norfolk's greatest-ever pace bowlers); Geoff and Eric Edrich; Jack Lingwood; George Langdale, who was turning out for Somerset; and Michael Barton.

Michael Falcon, although he was 58, was still in fine shape physically due to his daily exercise routine, and he decided to lead Norfolk for one last season in order to try to get them off to a good start in the post-war world. It was as well for Norfolk that he did decide to soldier on, as his scores of 70 not out and 30 in the first match of the season against Hertfordshire at Lakenham were largely responsible for setting up a comfortable victory, which turned out to be the sole win of the season. He was then rested for the second fixture,[61] before pottering around to little effect for the next three games: he then signed off from Minor Counties cricket with an unbeaten 44 as Norfolk amassed a big score in a draw against Cambridgeshire.

Surprisingly, Falcon was not the only player with experience of Minor Counties cricket before the Great War to appear after the Second World War. His old foe, Walter Franklin, who had first appeared in 1911, also played on for one more season for Buckinghamshire, aged 55. Even older than Falcon and Franklin was the great Buckinghamshire slow left-armer Frank Edwards, who had also played before the First World War. He was keen to resume his career, but his Committee were less enthusiatic and managed to limit him to one game in which rain prevented him from entering the field of play. (In passing, it is of note that only one player has performed effectively in the Minor Counties Championship at an age greater than that of Falcon's 58. He was, of course, Sydney Barnes who in 1932, at the age of 59, took 56 wickets at an average of only 9.01 for Staffordshire. That was his swan song, however for, although he played for a further three years, he suddenly lost his 'magic' and ceased to threaten at the Minor Counties level.)

Although two-day cricket put a bit of a strain on Michael Falcon physically, it would be incorrect to say that he was now 'past it'. He was still fit enough to play more or less a full season of Saturday afternoon fixtures and, whilst some were more social events than competitive matches, he put in a number of highly effective performances, securing at least three five-wicket returns. With the bat he was steady rather than commanding, but still finished second in the Norwich Wanderers' batting lists with an average of 23 or so. He was not a one-club man however, also turning out for

---

61   Harold Theobald took over the captaincy.

Norwich Union, Yarmouth and Norfolk Club and Ground. He was still playing for the sheer joy of it.

There remains to be dealt with the progress of Bill Edrich's brothers, Geoff and Eric, into the first-class game. According to Ralph Barker in *The Cricketing Family Edrich,* Geoff and Eric, anxious to emulate Bill (and another brother, Brian, who had obtained a contract with Kent), approached Michael Falcon for advice as to how to gain admittance to the first-class county game. His contacts had informed him that Lancashire were struggling desperately for players, so he wrote to Major Rupert Howard, the secretary at Old Trafford, and Geoff and Eric were duly signed up – without even having to leave Norfolk for a trial!

As well as stepping down from the Norfolk captaincy, Michael Falcon also resigned the chairmanship of the Yarmouth and Gorleston Conservative Association, being elected president upon standing down. The Association decided to cease supporting the local Liberal, Mr Jewson, and to put forward a candidate under the Conservative banner at the next election.

We should also note that Falcon's wife, Kathleen, was also active in the community's interest during the Second World War. Her daughter, Sybil, remembers that she did her share of shifts with the ARP in nearby Acle and she was also interested in the fortunes of St. Augustine's Lodge, a home for girls 'in trouble' (as it was then put) run by the Sisters of the Community of All Hallows, Ditchingham. The home was bombed and Kathleen Falcon was actively involved in the raising of funds to establish a new residence for the girls; several letters appeared in local newspapers from Mrs Falcon begging for support and then saying thank you for aid received.

Alf Mace

There are only two cricketers who remain alive today who played Minor Counties Championship cricket under the leadership of Michael Falcon. One of those is Alf Mace, who played most of his cricket in west Norfolk. He was something of a teenage prodigy and remembers averaging approximately 340 runs per innings in his final year at Sedgeford School, not far from Hunstanton. As a schoolboy he was advised by the county coach, Jack Nichols, to practise in front of a large mirror in the family home and monitor his backlift to ensure it remained straight.

Had it not been for the Second World War, during which Alf's work as a baker and in agriculture rendered him too valuable to be called up, he would probably have made his debut for Norfolk before 1946, when he was already 26 years old. Performing well in Club and Ground matches, Alf was duly rewarded with a call-up for the first Championship match of 1946, a fixture against Hertfordshire at Lakenham. In those days, before the mass ownership of motor cars, mobility was limited and petrol rationing during the War had worsened the situation so that cricketing communications between west Norfolk and the rest of the county were tenuous. Thus the first time Alf and Michael Falcon met was at the match itself. Furthermore, Falcon was unaware of Alf's capabilities. Alf remembers Falcon asking him where he batted and, when Alf replied that he was an opener, Falcon told him to go in at seven. (The scorecard reveals Alf's memory to be faulty as it shows him batting at five, one place above his skipper.) He also found himself fielding at third man and fine leg. Despite being treated as very much the junior, Alf has favourable memories of Falcon, remembering him as 'straightforward' and a 'marvellous man'. Although Falcon rebuked Alf for saying goodbye to his parents when he should have been padding up in the pavilion, Alf admits that he was the one in the wrong. He also remembers praise from Falcon whilst they were batting together; Alf faced a delivery which 'popped' and evaded it, causing Falcon to say, 'Well left, boy'.

Alf's career only really took off once Falcon had retired. He was one of the top batsmen in west Norfolk and played regularly with the Rought-Roughts, Wilfrid Thompson (whose Rolls-Royce he particularly remembers) and, at a later date, Norfolk slow left-armer Barry Battelley. Alf played for many sides: Toftrees (for whom he once accumulated 1,000 runs in a season, playing only on Saturdays), Fakenham, Wisbech, March and West Norfolk. His career statistics for Norfolk do not do him justice: seven matches yielded just 186 runs at an average of 16.91, with a highest score of 72. However his performances in club cricket were sufficiently impressive for Leicestershire to invite him for a trial, and even to get as far as arranging accommodation for Alf at Hinckley. Unfortunately he broke his leg playing football shortly before the trial and the injury took a couple of years to heal properly. By this time he was too old for Leicestershire still to be interested, nor did Norfolk invite him to play again despite his continuing to dominate club cricket in the western half of the county.

Chapter Eight
Life After Big-Time Cricket

Following his forty years as a player, there was now a brief hiatus in Falcon's involvement with Norfolk C.C.C. To mark his services to Norfolk cricket there was, in 1947, a presentation to him in front of the Lakenham pavilion of a portrait of himself painted by Oswald Birley,[62] contributions to which were made by no fewer than 240 subscribers. This portrait is still owned by Michael Falcon's son.

After a couple of years rest, Michael Falcon was appointed chairman of Norfolk C.C.C. in 1950 and continued in this role until 1969 when he stood down, only to be elected as president for the next three years. Committee records for this period have not survived and so his loyal spadework has gone unrecorded, save from the odd glimpse in the *Eastern Daily Press* sports columns. To

Michael Falcon at the Norwich Union's 150th anniversary dinner in 1958.

mark his services to the club, the committee opened a subscription list for a presentation which he chose to take in the form of two large wooden benches, suitably inscribed, which were installed in front of the pavilion at Lakenham. When the club moved to Manor Park, Horsford, in 2001 the benches were left behind, in error. The landlord proved to be somewhat reluctant to let the benches go and it was only after a threat of legal action that the benches were released and installed on the new ground.

Michael Falcon continued his involvement with the Norwich Union, started before the death of his father,

---

62   Birley was a leading portrait painter of this period, well-known for his paintings of the royal family and war-time leaders. He painted several well-regarded portraits of his friend Sir Winston Churchill, and gave him lessons. Eight years older than Falcon, he had also attended Harrow School and Cambridge University. He was knighted in 1949.

continuing as a director of both the Life Insurance Society and the Fire Society until he became vice-president of the Life Insurance Society in 1948 and of the Fire Society in 1958. He retired from both boards in July 1963, upon reaching the age limit. Falcon also remained active in the management of the Yarmouth-based brewery E.Lacon and Co Ltd. He continued as chairman until 1963 and, after he had stepped down from that office, continued as a non-executive director for some time afterwards.

Unsurprisingly, Michael Falcon's retirement from county cricket merely opened the way for him to play more social cricket. He played into his seventies, enjoying his successes at a lower level every bit as much as he enjoyed first-class cricket in his salad days. His son remembers him particularly enjoying a friendly match against Gresham's School at Holt. Falcon was fielding contentedly in the deep as a talented batsman who had got his eye in was looking to push on to a notable score. At this point his captain offered Falcon a bowl: the batsman, seeing what appeared to be a harmless old man coming on to bowl, couldn't believe his luck and decided to cash in by hitting as many runs as possible before the old boy was taken off. The first ball was of impeccable line and length but no more than slow-medium in pace and the young batsman unscientifically carted it over the boundary for a six. Michael Falcon considered his options. His days of sheer pace were forty years before; even outswing and inswing were but distant memories. His only weapon was the use of subtle variation in his delivery; so, from an identical run-up, he delivered a ball slightly different from the first. The batsman, who by now was so completely sure of himself that he didn't notice the subtle change, played exactly the same shot which had been so successful against Falcon's first ball. This time, however, the variation did the trick: the bat missed the ball completely and the ball went on to hit the wicket. The boy slouched off in high disgust, completely unaware of the calibre of his victorious foe, who enjoyed himself immensely.

At one point, which is now impossible to date, Michael Falcon's cricketing days were threatened by a medical condition which resulted in his hands becoming involuntarily contracted into fists, making normal day-to-day functioning tricky and cricket impossible. Luckily surgery proved successful, with one hand being corrected one year and the other in the following year. Cricket was then resumed as soon as possible.

Some matches were, of course, more important than others: four stand out from the crowd. These were the All-Edrich XI *v* G.E.Pilch's XI, in 1947; Norfolk *v* F.G.Mann's XI, in 1951; Norfolk XI *v* the All-Edrich XI, in 1955; and M.Falcon's XI *v* Norwich Union, in 1959.

In the match between the All-Edrich XI and George Pilch's XI in September 1947, played in front of a crowd of 4,500, Eric Edrich made one of the splendid centuries that all too infrequently graced his career. His 129 contained five sixes and 12 fours and led to a total of 283 for 6 declared. The bowlers' figures suffered, with the honourable exception of Michael Falcon who, receiving a fine welcome from the crowd when he took the ball, returned figures of 18-8-29-3, Eric Edrich being among his victims.

In the second match, arranged in celebration of the Festival of Britain, George Mann (son of Falcon's old team-mate Frank Mann) turned up at Lakenham with ten men due to a late call-off and asked Falcon if he fancied a game, an invitation which of course was accepted. Falcon was not needed to bat in Mann's first innings but, when Norfolk had their knock, Mann brought him on as second change. Again being greeted with a warm ovation from the crowd, Falcon produced some steady bowling, returning figures of 12-2-42-1. In Mann's XI second innings Falcon was promoted to four, being accorded another ovation. He made only nine, but one drive through the covers brought back memories.

*F.G.Mann's XI against Norfolk, with one E.W.Swanton at the crease, in a
Festival of Britain match at Lakenham in 1951.
Falcon played for Mann's side as a 'last-minute' call-up.*

In the match between the Norfolk XI and the All-Edrich XI in 1955, organised as part of Geoff Edrich's benefit, Bill Edrich finally showed a Norfolk audience the full range of his talent. He scored an unbeaten 167 out of a total of 221 for 9 declared. Among the heavy scoring, Falcon's bowling still had a command of line and length and he conceded only 13 runs from his eight overs. Going into bat at eight, after an upper-order collapse, he joined another Norfolk stalwart from before the war, Frank Cunliffe, and they added 81 runs for the sixth wicket, thereby saving the game. Falcon's share was an unbeaten 37 which contained several powerful drives through the covers.

Perhaps the final important match in Michael Falcon's 'social' cricket career occurred in 1959, at the age of 71, when he captained an eleven against Norwich Union in celebration of the opening of the new pavilion at the club's ground at Pinebanks. The match, which was ruined by rain – Falcon neither batted nor bowled – was notable in that Falcon's side contained no fewer than six Norfolk captains, past, present and future. Apart from Falcon himself, the past captains were Wilfrid Thompson (1947-1950); Laurie Barrett (1951-1954); and Peter Powell (1955-1958). The 'present' captain was the then newly-appointed Bill Edrich (1959-1968); and the future captain was the Repton schoolboy David Pilch (1972-1975).

Just one last match.
Michael Falcon, at the age of 71, led this side, including six Norfolk captains, at the opening of the new Norwich Union sports ground in 1959.

In 1969 Michael Falcon reappeared in the cricketing spotlight as the author of a closely argued article on the subject of spin bowling, published in *The Cricketer*. It showed a mind still sharp and incisive at the age of 81: it was as many as 55 years since he had been co-opted onto the MCC Committee prior to the Great War. In 1971 he was asked to present the caps, at Norwich, to the English Schools Under-15 side when, as was reported by George Chesterton and Hubert Doggart in *Oxford and Cambridge Cricket*, he was 'the same courteous and friendly person that his contemporaries had known.'

In his old age, Falcon successfully overcame cancer, but when he and Kathleen moved from North Burlingham to 10 Cathedral Close, Norwich, he was still not very mobile. He developed the habit of taking a walk around the Close every day; his daughter Sybil remembers the soft green turf of the Norwich Grammar School playing fields which would have provided a suitably forgiving surface on which to walk. His quality of life soon improved and before long he was taking an interest in the cricket being played by the schoolboys in the Lower Close, where his old team-mate 'Bozzy' Boswell was groundsman. He became friends with his next-door neighbour, Peter Harrison, who ran the Grammar School boarding house for 8-12 year olds and they would frequently chat over the garden fence.[63] Peter Harrison remembers Michael Falcon as a very congenial companion, articulate to the last and full of memories of his 'golden days'. Unsurprisingly, Sydney Barnes had left a lasting mark on Falcon's memory and he also recalled playing with Gilbert Jessop and 'Plum' Warner. He would also converse with the boys, sometimes delaying their departure from the nets in the direction of the refectory for their tea: in mitigation they would plead that the old man was so interesting that they had lost track of time.

Peter Harrison's son George was presented one birthday with a brand new cricket ball which he treated with reverence and kept in a pristine condition. Another gift, highly valued by Peter, was Michael Falcon's barrister's wig which must have been over fifty years old. Falcon was an avid viewer of Test cricket on television; Sybil recalls her father sitting on an upright chair, up close to the

---

63 I too was a pupil of Peter Harrison at the relevant time, but as a day-boy not a boarder, and so did not attend after-school nets. To think that I got so close to meeting the man who, in researching this book, I have come to consider as Norfolk's finest and most loyal citizen, is intensely frustrating.

screen, taking great pleasure in being able to watch the action from behind the bowler's arm.

Although he had long ceased to be active in political life, Michael Falcon retained an interest in current affairs and politics to the end. He also remained interested in the organisation of Norfolk cricket. At meetings of bodies such as the Norfolk Cricket Association he had regularly stressed the importance of sporting facilities and recognition of his work behind the scenes as vice-chairman of the Norfolk County Playing Fields Association executive committee came in 1974, when he was presented by Prince Philip with the National Playing Fields Association's President's Certificate at Buckingham Palace.

Michael Falcon opening the new Lacon's bowling green in 1960.

Michael Falcon died on 27 February 1976, aged 87, and was blessed with a quick, painless death. He was sitting up at home when a locum doctor, paying him a first visit, made the mistake of mispronouncing his patient's name, rendering the 'FAL' in Falcon as in 'fallacy'. Falcon testily replied to the effect that his name was pronounced with the 'FAL' in Falcon as in 'fall' – and promptly expired. This amused his wife Kathleen to a degree that it eased the pain of his passing: his son, Michael Gascoigne, also remembers the story fondly.

His funeral took place at Norwich Cathedral. The Dean of Norwich, the Very Rev Alan Webster, paid tribute to Michael Falcon's humanity, good humour and sense of duty, declaring 'He was always a delight to meet, talking about Test cricket and gardening problems, and was a regular and appreciative member of the Cathedral congregation, popular with young and old.' Bryan Stevens, an old team-mate and cricket correspondent of the *Eastern Daily Press,* recalled that, even in his old age, Falcon was a regular spectator at Lakenham, watching the game from his own tent and usually accompanied by his wife. Although he was prone to reminisce about the days of yore, as most elderly men are, he thoroughly enjoyed watching Norfolk play the modern game.[64]

---

64 In recognition of his unique service to Norfolk cricket, both Falcon and his wife Kathleen were made honorary life vice-presidents of Norfolk CCC; they were the only people accorded that honour. After Falcon died, Kathleen continued to be so honoured until she died in 1985.

Chapter Nine
A Test Cricketer?

When one reads reports of the first-class career of Michael Falcon it soon becomes commonplace to read that, given regular county cricket with a first-class background, he could have had a Test career. For instance, Peter Wynne-Thomas in *Who's Who of Cricketers* wrote of him: 'One of the greatest of regular Minor Counties cricketers, he might have played for England if he had appeared more often in first-class cricket.' Again, David Armstrong, in *Barclays World of Cricket*, suggested: 'Many thought him good enough to have played Test cricket if he had qualified for a first-class county.' In *Who's Won The Toss?*, E.H.D.Sewell stated: 'Had he been playing regularly then for a first-class county instead of for Norfolk, we should find "Mike" Falcon's name frequently on both sides of the Test match ledger and that not the debit side. For he was also a very useful stroke-playing batsman with a sound style, and had the physique for the job.' David Lemmon and Douglas Smith, in *Votes for Cricket*, thought that 'Falcon has a record in first-class cricket which suggests that if he had given himself fully to the game, he would have been an outstanding player. As it was, he chose to play his cricket for his beloved Norfolk, a decision which almost certainly cost him international recognition.' In *Bill Edrich: A Biography*, Alan Hill stated: 'He was regarded by many good judges as possessing England credentials had he appeared more often in first-class cricket.'[65]

The call to play first-class county cricket did come. In conversations with his son and with Peter Harrison, Falcon himself implicated both Frank Mann and 'Plum' Warner in offering him the possibility of a Test cap and maybe even the captaincy, as a

---

[65] An outcome of his determination to play for Norfolk is that he holds a curious record. No English-born and resident cricketer appeared in more first-class games in the British Isles in the twentieth century without playing in the County Championship. As can be seen in the Appendix, he played 89 first-class matches, all in England. Three other players exceeded fifty: Walter Franklin with 60; Joseph Comber with 56; and Neville Tufnell, who played some of his county cricket for Norfolk, 55. Tufnell, a wicket-keeper, also played 15 matches overseas, including one Test in South Africa in 1910.

temptation to get him to qualify for Middlesex by residence. He wasn't interested however, preferring to play for his beloved Norfolk. It's not that he had any dislike of the toughness with which Test cricket was played: indeed he showed an appreciation of the combative attitudes of the Australians, as would be expected of one who went head-to-head on a regular basis with the likes of Sydney Barnes and Walter Franklin. The *Eastern Daily Press* referred on several occasions to the 'edge' in games Norfolk played with Staffordshire and Buckinghamshire. Though no doubt short of Test matches in import, they were still fiercely fought contests.

Some sources go further in pushing Michael Falcon's claim to international recognition. To quote from the obituary by R.L.Arrowsmith in *Wisden*, Michael Falcon was ' ... a cricketer who might well have played in Test matches had he been qualified for a first-class county. As it was, there were those who thought that he would have strengthened the deplorably weak English bowling in 1921 ...'. In *The Cricketer* in 1958 Edward Knight stated: 'In the Test matches of 1921, when some panic selections led to the appearance of 30 players for England against W.W.Armstrong's wonderful side, Falcon might well have been tried for his country.' Archie MacLaren, also writing in *The Cricketer* in 1921, when Falcon was still playing, declared: 'It strikes me as a pity that such a class bowler as Michael Falcon should have had no opportunity to show that he bowls as well as ever ... . In my opinion he is the best fast bowler we have, and would have been very awkward on some of our fast wickets.' MacLaren duly plucked Falcon from obscurity and, as described in Chapter Five, selected him to open the bowling against the 1921 Australians, being rewarded with a match-winning performance. Those unfamiliar with MacLaren's later days might think that the old warrior's selection of Falcon was another sudden discovery akin to his choice of Sydney Barnes for the Ashes tour of 1901/02. This was not the case: after his virtual retirement from first-class cricket, MacLaren entered the employment of Lionel Robinson, a wealthy Australian who built a splendid ground at Old Buckenham, deep in the Norfolk countryside. The ex-England skipper raised and captained elevens – some of first-class standard – to play friendly cricket to keep Robinson amused, and propped up the bar in his spare time. He had plenty of opportunity to observe Michael Falcon in action for Norfolk, so that it is clear that he was not an instant 'discovery', but a cricketer on whom MacLaren had been keeping his eyes for several years. If MacLaren had been a selector, Michael Falcon would have won a Test cap regardless of his county status. In support of this most favourable view of Falcon was Rowland Ryder, writing in *Cricket Calling*, who stated bluntly and without qualification: 'Michael Falcon was a player of test match calibre who played for his native Norfolk.'

Sympathy for Falcon's status was found, again, in *The Cricketer.* 'Any really great cricketers, like Barnes or Michael Falcon, who happen to play for a Minor County, should have their claims especially considered if they happen to be great bowlers.' Being bracketed with Sydney Barnes as a 'great' bowler is praise indeed! A comparison with Barnes was also noted by E.M.Wellings in *Vintage Cricketers,* who described Falcon as ' ... a splendid opening bowler who, like Barnes, played most of his more important cricket in the Minor County Championship for Norfolk, but was also good enough for Gentlemen v Players matches at Lord's.' It was in these fixtures between the Gentlemen and the Players that one discovers the one fly in Michael Falcon's ointment: his 41 wickets in these fixtures, ranking just below Test status, cost as many runs as 31.08 each. *Wisden* opined that 'he had moreover a knack of producing his best form on important occasions': although he did have his successes against the Players, taking six for 58 in 1913 (including the last five wickets for eight runs in 3.2 overs), five for 157 in 1920 and seven for 78 in 1924 (all at The Oval), his record overall in these fixtures would tend to contradict *Wisden* and suggest that, at the very top level, he fell just short.

However, consideration of Falcon's performances against touring teams contradicts the view that he lacked the vital spark that would have enabled him to compete at the very highest level and backs up *Wisden.* Mention has been made of his many feats against the visiting elevens, so only a brief recapitulation will be made to highlight the fact that Michael Falcon regularly got the better of the tourists whenever he was allowed to meet them when in his prime. In 1909, at a stage in his career when he was a batsman, he top-scored with 46 for Cambridge University against the Australians. In 1911, he took five for 50 against the Indians to condemn them to defeat against the Light Blues. In 1912, his return of six for 47 against the South Africans helped dismiss the tourists for just 151. In 1919, Falcon and Johnny Douglas bowled out the Australian Forces for just 85, with Falcon's share being six for 41. In 1921, of course, his six for 67 played a vital role in Archie MacLaren's win at Eastbourne. Three years later he took three for

48 and five for 103 as he captained the Minor Counties side to victory against a near Test-strength South African XI. Finally, in 1926, on an unhelpfully slow pitch, he took seven for 42 for the Minor Counties to dismiss the Australians for 179, albeit in a non first-class fixture. The Australians certainly had a healthy dislike of facing Michael Falcon's bowling. After his AIF side were routed, Herbie Collins told 'Plum' Warner that he had never played more difficult fast bowling than Falcon's on that day. Going on to be similarly demolished in 1921, the Australians were, according to Warner writing in the *Morning Post*, 'unanimously of the opinion that Falcon was much the best fast bowler they had encountered that season'.

The record is clear: put Michael Falcon in his prime up against a touring eleven and you would probably be rewarded with a game-swinging performance. (In his later years Falcon was sometimes a bit of passenger against touring teams but he retained the proud record of never losing to a touring side whilst playing in a first-class fixture.) To quote *The Cricketer* again, 'He may certainly consider himself unfortunate in not having represented England in this country so far' and 'We believe Michael Falcon to be the most difficult bowler in England. He has pace, he can make the ball swing away from the bat, and he can also send down a nasty off-break.' This last quote dates from 1924 when Falcon was 36 and, one would have thought, past his prime as a new-ball bowler, but he was supremely fit and still causing havoc against Minor County batsmen.

And then, out of the blue, the call came. Michael Falcon was asked to make himself available for the 1924/25 MCC tour of Australia. According to C.B.L.Prior, speaking of Falcon at the annual dinner of the Norwich Wanderers Cricket Club, ' ... he had the opportunity of going to Australia last year, and if he had not been such a busy man, Norfolk would have had a representative in the MCC team.' E.H.D.Sewell – admittedly a man of strong and sometimes heterodox views – opined that Falcon would have done well down under, saying that 'Falcon could have been backed both ways to bring home the bacon from Australia, where his cheerful, strong, and virile personality was ideal for such a long tour.' (In passing, it is of interest that, whilst Maurice Tate bowled wonderfully well throughout the trip, he received negligible support from the other pace bowlers on tour. Falcon would have almost certainly been ideal back-up to Tate.) Prior also praised Michael Falcon for his loyalty and splendid service to Norfolk cricket, recalling him making that overnight journey from Ireland in order to represent Norfolk in the Minor County Championship in 1910. Modest to the last, Falcon spoke little if at all about the missed opportunity to represent MCC. In being a 'part-time' player, unable to tour owing to business commitments, he found himself in the same position as contemporary amateurs Clem Gibson and Walter Franklin, both of whom had to turn down invitations to join Ashes touring parties. (Gibson had business interests in Argentina, where he was born, and Franklin had an active legal practice.)

It has been suggested that the Great War hampered Michael Falcon's chances of selection for a home Test. Superficially the argument has merit: in 1915 Falcon was 27, in his prime for a bowler who was faster than just fast-medium. Gilbert Jessop, in *A Cricketer's Log*, commented: 'The success of "Mike" Falcon caused me no surprise, for I had seen him in the previous season skittle Yorkshire out at Scarborough [in 1912], his handiwork being 5 wickets for 16. He was genuinely fast without being quite so "pacey" as Neville Knox or Hitch, and with the new ball his swerving proclivities made him a particularly undesirable customer to face.' E.H.D.Sewell described Falcon as being 'above fast-medium pace' and went on to describe his bowling favourably:

> Falcon had an ideal high action, did not reduce his value by checking at delivery, and had good command at pitching the away-swerve where the batsman does not like it to pitch, *i.e.* if missed by the bat the ball hit the wicket, and not too often the wicket-keeper. Owing to his pace and action he was also able to produce that highest proof of good fast bowling, the good length ball that gets up sharply.

As if in agreement, Herbie Collins 'was heard to remark in 1919 that his [Falcon's] bowling was yards faster than any they had met during the whole of their tour' but by then he was 31 and theoretically a little old for a paceman, although his bowling for Norfolk in 1920 was as hostile, parsimonious and well-rewarded as that of Sydney Barnes. *The Times* stated that he bowled faster against the Australian Forces in 1919 than he had ever bowled prior to the Great War. However, deeper analysis refutes this viewpoint. If there had been no war, the triumvirate of fast-medium bowlers who had destroyed Australia in 1911/12 would still have been available for selection. Johnny Douglas, Frank Foster and Sydney Barnes were a formidable combination who would likely have kept Michael Falcon out of contention for a Test place. As it was, there was a war, during which Foster's first-class career was ended by a motor-cycle crash in which he broke both legs, and after which the selectors decided that Barnes was too old for further Test matches. Furthermore, an accomplished fast-medium bowler from Yorkshire, Major Booth, who had played Tests in South Africa, failed to survive the war, as did Percy Jeeves, a highly promising all-rounder who played for Warwickshire and who had impressed 'Plum' Warner so much that he had predicted a Test career for the youngster. (Falcon also noted Jeeves' talent when they were opposed in a Gentlemen *v* Players fixture at The Oval, being quoted by Rowland Ryder as saying: 'Hullo, here's someone!')

The overall effect of the Great War was thus, unexpectedly, to advance Michael Falcon to a position where the selectors could (and should) have given him a chance in 1921, three years ahead of his actual opportunity. The pacemen England selected to play Test cricket over the period at which Falcon was at his peak had a very sorry record: Bill Hitch, Harry Howell and Abe Waddington played 14 Tests between them, taking a pitiful 15 wickets in total at a combined average of an extortionate 66.87 runs apiece.

Claims for Michael Falcon can go further than a mere Test place, however: he has a claim to be considered as a potential captain of the Test team. Johnny Douglas, despite winning the 1911/12 Ashes series and being a brave trier, was not much of a captain: he was both a poor man-motivator and a poor tactician who often overbowled himself. Recognising his limitations, the selectors offered the captaincy of the 1920/21 Ashes tour to Reggie Spooner and Douglas was only appointed when the Lancashire amateur had to decline the invitation. As is well known, Douglas lost the series 5-0 and then, when hostilities resumed in England, he started by losing two more Tests against the seemingly unstoppable Australians. The selectors (Spooner, Henry Foster and John Daniell) who did a collective impression of a headless chicken all summer, selecting no fewer than 30 players for the five Tests, correctly deposed Douglas, who was by now irretrievably damaged goods.

Here was the chance to do what Archie MacLaren was suggesting: strengthen the pace attack by bringing in Michael Falcon and, what's more, bring him in as skipper. His captaincy of Norfolk had already attracted favourable notice: 'Falcon handled his side and arranged his bowling wonderfully well throughout the game,' said MacLaren of the Norfolk man's captaincy against Staffordshire in 1913. If they had had a crystal ball, the selectors would have seen more evidence that Michael Falcon was a gifted leader of men. His defeat of the near full-strength 1924 South Africans, with only the resources of the Minor Counties to call on, showed he could skipper at the highest level and in the Minor Counties Championship his captaincy was consistently innovative and was praised frequently in the local press. It may be pushing things too far to see a Minor County cricketer skippering an Ashes Test, but Michael Falcon 'captain of Middlesex and England' is, in hindsight, an entirely plausible response to Armstrong's 1921 Australians. By 1914, however, it was only ever going to be Michael Falcon 'captain of Norfolk' and he was more than content with the honour of leading his native county.

As it was, the panic-stricken selectors turned to the aged C.B.Fry, who declined the offer to skipper himself, but talked them into appointing Lionel Tennyson to replace Douglas. Tennyson, like Douglas was brave, but was considerably more clueless even than his predecessor, as his illegal declaration in the Old Trafford Test showed. As it turned out, the selectors were lucky: when Tennyson badly split his left hand whilst fielding in the Headingley Test, he showed his bravery by scoring, in two innings, 99 runs, some with one hand using a junior bat, and England did become invigorated and then put up more of a fight. (David Lemmon, though, attributed England's improved performance to Australian apathy once the series had been decided.) Although he was cheerful in adversity, Tennyson was wayward, eccentric and had a heavy gambling habit. He was in many ways an accident waiting to happen, quite unsuitable as an England skipper, and the selectors duly dispensed with him as soon as The Ashes series was over, before he had chance to drop too many bricks.

Michael Falcon, an MP of three years Commons' experience – we can imagine the headline 'Tory MP to captain England' – would have embarrassed nobody by his behaviour if he had been appointed Test skipper. We can be sure though, that to Falcon himself, it wouldn't have been as enjoyable as playing for Norfolk: in 1928, during one of his many speeches of thanks upon his re-election as Norfolk skipper, Falcon declared that he enjoyed playing for Norfolk more than anything else. By way of finishing this flight-of-fancy, comparison of his first-class career averages

with those of the gentlemen who captained England between
C.B.Fry in 1912 and Arthur Carr in 1926 reveals that Michael
Falcon would not have been out of his depth as a contributor with
bat or ball if he had skippered in that era:

	Batting Avge	Bowling Avge
J.W.H.T.Douglas	27.90	23.32
Hon L.H.Tennyson	23.33	54.10
F.T.Mann	23.42	83.00
A.E.R.Gilligan	20.08	23.20
M.Falcon	25.24	24.79

Douglas has marginally the best figures but, as has already been
argued, he was a busted flush by June 1921. None of the others
were any more successful than Michael Falcon at the first-class
game. Lest it be thought that Falcon's figures were artificially
improved by his many appearances for the Free Foresters against
Cambridge and Oxford Universities, the statistics clearly refute
this: he suffered some of his severest beatings as a bowler when
turning out against the Universities. On the contrary, it was the
others who had their statistics artificially massaged in two
separate ways. Firstly, they all had the advantage of being captains
of first-class counties. In those days many umpires, who were of
very low status, were well known to give the benefit of any doubt in
a decision involving a captain in his favour in the hope that he
would look kindly upon them when marking them in his match
report. For example, Cyril Washbrook has been reported as saying
that the captaincy of Lancashire was worth 400 runs a season.[66] A
little massaging would have done Michael Falcon's statistics no
harm: and by the way, no evidence exists that the same sort of
thing went on in the Minor Counties Championship. Secondly, the
others had the chance to improve their figures by playing against
lowly counties such as Derbyshire, Worcestershire, Northamptonshire, Leicestershire and Glamorgan whose resistance in those
days varied between the spirited-but-outgunned to the token. By
comparison, if Falcon's weakest opponents in the first-class game
were the Universities, his figures were bound to suffer in
comparison.

---

66   Notable exceptions amongst the umpires were Frank Chester and Cec Pepper,
who were known to be fearless and impartial. As far as I know, there has been
no statistical investigation of the phenomenon of the 'cowardly umpire', but it
remains part of the folklore of the first-class game.

Chapter Ten
Michael Falcon's Legacy

As has been seen, Michael Falcon did not always put Norfolk cricket first. He missed the entire 1909 Minor Counties season and thereafter the odd game in favour of playing for the Harrow Wanderers, the Gentlemen and, most surprisingly, the Incogniti in 1913. However his loyalty quickly hardened and he did, in effect, sacrifice any higher ambition in favour of his native county after the Great War. His record in the Minor Counties Championship is truly remarkable. Uniquely, he captained his county before the First World War and after the Second World War; he was the leading run scorer at the time of his retirement, and would still be if his career had not been interrupted by both World Wars; and he was one of the leading wicket-takers of all time, again losing opportunities due to the Great War.

In the Minor Counties Handbook of 2000, edited by Mike Berry, a 'Team of the Century' was put forward, and whilst this made no claim to be the final word on the matter of the greatest Minor Counties cricketers, it is more or less the sole word at the present time. Mike Berry, described selection to the team as 'rewarding longevity of service and [picking] those who scored the most runs and took the most wickets over those who were arguably superior in technique but whose careers were fleeting by way of comparison.' (Presumably this explains the absence of stalwart players such as George Thompson of Northamptonshire, who went on to play Test cricket, but the omission of Bill Edrich, who scored 8,034 runs and took 415 wickets for Norfolk in the Championship, is harder to justify.) Regardless of who may have been left out, Falcon justifiably found a place in the team as a true all-rounder, worth his place as a batsman and a fast bowler; unarguably his service was long and his technique was superior. Perhaps it was also intended that he would be skipper, too.

The table below lists the players selected for the 'Team of the Century' and gives details of their careers in 'competitive' Minor Counties matches.

Minor Counties Championship: 'Team of the Century' Career Details

	Batting		Bowling	
	Runs	*Ave*	*Wkt*	*Ave*
Mike Nurton (Oxfordshire)	12713	33.36	7	39.43
Arthur Sutton (Cheshire)	10540	28.64	435	20.23
Nick Folland (Devon)	10132	51.69	26	37.80
Charles Titchmarsh (Herts)	10517	37.97	1	75.00
Stephen Plumb (Norfolk, Lincs)	12266	41.86	328	32.32
Michael Falcon (Norfolk)	11538	33.84	690	16.52
D.W. 'Bill' Stokes (Berkshire)	5365	25.18	1	51.00
Sydney Barnes (Staffordshire)	4806	21.36	1376	7.99
Cyril Perkins (Suffolk)	2044	15.36	779	13.34
Fred Burton (Hertfordshire)	1894	11.14	1051	17.04
Frank Edwards (Surrey II, Bucks)	1099	8.20	1059	11.06

Notes: The details given relate to performances in the Minor Counties Championship only. Stokes was selected as the wicket-keeper; he took 177 catches and made 77 stumpings in the competition. The figures for Nurton, Titchmarsh, Burton, Stokes and Barnes were kindly provided by Julian Lawton Smith, Bob Simons, Roy New, Tony Webb and Tony Percival. Figures for Perkins and Edwards derive from the books written by Colin Munford and Douglas Miller listed in the bibliography at the end of this book. Those for Sutton, Folland and Plumb are from the Minor Counties Handbooks of 1987, 2002 and 2003. The figures for Falcon are from the author's research. As the ACS Minor Counties project progresses, some of these figures may, of course, be corrected.

Falcon as All-Rounder

It is apparent from the table that Falcon was selected as an all-rounder. So how much of an all-rounder was he? Sometimes it is stated that a quantitative measure of an all-rounder is a player whose batting average is higher than his bowling average. For purposes of comparison between all-rounders, dividing an individual's batting average by his bowling average yields a number which will be referred to as his 'ratio' and which gives an indication of the relative effectiveness of that all-rounder; the higher the ratio, the more outstanding the all-rounder. Falcon's batting and bowling averages in the Minor Counties Championship are 33.84 and 16.52 respectively; giving a ratio of 2.05. This is a great achievement over such an extremely long career, matched by very few others at this level; one who does measure up is Sydney Barnes, whose career bowling average is so low that his modest batting average is sufficiently high to qualify. None of the other batsmen in the 'Team of the Century' (Charles Titchmarsh, Arthur Sutton, Mike Nurton, Stephen Plumb or Nick Folland) have been bowlers who spearheaded the attack. Arthur Sutton's 435 wickets were taken at 20.23 each whilst Stephen Plumb's 328 wickets cost an expensive 32.32 runs apiece. Michael Falcon stands out in Minor Counties history as one of the greatest all-rounders and certainly the longest lasting.[67]

It is Falcon's status as an amateur that marks him out as a special case amongst the bowlers. When he started his Minor Counties career, he wasn't required to bowl as Norfolk, like almost all other counties, had professionals to do the bulk of the bowling. Norfolk had relied on Billy Smith and Ted Gibson to take the wickets for several years: indeed the county had to drop out of the Minor Counties Championship in 1902 and 1903, while Smith and Gibson were qualifying to play for Norfolk by residence. When Michael Falcon took over, leading the attack until his powers began to wane in the late 1920s, he was, as an amateur, very much an oddity. This is not to say that other amateurs did not bowl well for Norfolk; slow left armer Walter Beadsmoore and paceman Rodney Rought-Rought both performed nobly between the Wars but Falcon was the spearhead of the attack. All the other bowlers in the 'Team of the Century' were professionals (Fred Burton, Frank Edwards, Cyril Perkins and Sydney Barnes) and only Barnes was a force with the bat.

In this respect it is worth noting that Falcon himself, writing in *The Cricketer* in 1939 in reply to a discussion by George H.Wood on the all-rounder in cricket, insisted that 'the definition of an all-rounder is too narrow if it does not include ability to field with consistency, safety, and even distinction in almost any position in the field.' By

---

67   Of other highly-regarded all-rounders George Thompson posts a highly impressive ratio of 2.67 in his Minor County Championship career, but unlike those of Michael Falcon, his figures do not 'suffer' from his playing to an advanced age; he was only 28 when he last played in the Championship. If Michael Falcon had retired at the age of 40 – not a bad age for a pace bowler – he would have finished with a ratio of 2.53, which, to invite hyperbole, would have been an incredibly high value and indicative of his dominance of the Minor Counties cricket scene. Bill Edrich's ratio is marginally less impressive at 1.83 but, of course, he played Minor County cricket only in his youth and in his cricketing old age – if he had remained devoted to Norfolk like Falcon, and played for his native county during his pomp, his ratio would probably surpass that of his first captain. The attainment of a career ratio of 2.00 or above is similarly rare in the first-class game. Unsurprisingly, W.G.Grace qualifies comfortably, but a number of supremely talented all-rounders such as Wilfred Rhodes and George Hirst fall short of the stringent target, whilst Frank Woolley only just achieves the benchmark. It would appear to be easier for prominent all-rounders to dominate in Australia: Warwick Armstrong, Charlie Macartney and Keith Miller all comfortably exceed the ratio of 2.00.

all accounts, Michael Falcon's fielding qualified him as an all-rounder even by his strict standards, although to judge from *Wisden* he sometimes had difficulty securing good catching from his charges. The only fielding position where he would have had limited experience for Norfolk was first slip, which was the domain of Geoffrey Stevens for as long as he played.

In David Armstrong's excellent *Short History of Norfolk Cricket* he has a chapter title mentioning 'The Legend'. He is referring to his childhood hero, Bill Edrich, who certainly led by example and his captaincy certainly had an invigorating effect on a side that had been in the doldrums for several years. In contrast, when Philip Yaxley uses the term 'legend' as a sub-heading in his equally meritorious *Looking Back at Norfolk Cricket,* it is to Michael Falcon that he is referring. To place one of these two above the other would be invidious and it would perhaps be fairest to describe them both as 'legends', giving invaluable service to Norfolk cricket.[68] Their performances as players and captains for Norfolk were both highly exemplary, although of course Edrich's best years were in the first-class and Test games, whilst Falcon remained loyal to Norfolk throughout his career. Falcon also spent many years doing patient spadework on the Committee, something which was not Edrich's forte. Bill Edrich himself, writing in his heyday of 1947, describes the help Michael Falcon gave to him as a youngster and, in doing so, confirms Falcon's place as an all-time great in Norfolk cricket:

> He was, of all the cricketers I have known, one of the most unselfish, courageous and inspiring. Without his leadership, backed as it always was by really magnificent all-round cricket, I do not know whether the Norfolk club could have survived at anything like the standard it attained. Without him, many boys now ranking as fine cricketers would never have had the chance to display their talents. He worked over novices untiringly, year

---

68   Would it be heretical to name George Raikes as a third 'legend'? After an inauspicious start as a stop-gap wicket-keeper to replace Rev Archdale Wickham (who left to play for Somerset), he developed into a highly effective all-rounder. An aggressive batsman and a bowler of slow leg-breaks, his appearances for Norfolk were limited by his clerical duties so that his career aggregates do not stand comparison with those of Falcon or Edrich. However, when he did find time to skipper his county, his performances were, as has been mentioned in Chapter Two, instrumental in leading Norfolk to two Minor Counties Championships. Given that Falcon was actually in the United States when the title was won in 1913, it can be said that Raikes won two more Championships than the other two 'legends' combined!

in and year out, his only hope of reward being that one day the boys would enjoy the best cricket they had it in them to give.

Edrich went further: 'He had the eye of a true falcon for any promising young cricketer, and nothing was too much for him to do so that the game he loved should benefit if the green youngster could be turned to something better ... he patiently coached and advised me, helped and encouraged me.'

Bill Edrich and Michael Falcon were as one in agreeing that cricket was a game to be played for fun. To quote from Edrich's biographer, Alan Hill: 'For the crowds flocking back to Lakenham, said "Jim" Swanton, Edrich's daring tactical approach struck a vein of reminiscence in accord with the exploits of his first county captain, Michael Falcon, in the great days between the wars.' They were also alike in the loyalty and affection they generated in their team-mates – the relationship between Michael Falcon and his players has already been touched upon but, again, Bill Edrich throws further light on affairs: 'none of us wanted reputation for itself that summer [1933]; we were absolutely set on getting the Championship, and mainly because we wanted Michael Falcon to have the thrill of leading us home after so many gallant attempts.'

It should not be thought however that, popular with their men as they were, either Michael Falcon or Bill Edrich were soft touches as captains. Both set high standards and woe betide any team member who failed to live up to them. David Armstrong remembers that Bill would not tolerate chatterboxes in his eleven, whilst Peter Harrison recalls Michael Falcon telling him that, on one occasion, a player turned up wearing muddy boots rather than the pristine white footwear demanded by his captain – as a punishment the scruffily-shod miscreant was banished to the third-man boundary at both ends for the duration of the innings.

As an aside, it is of interest that these two stalwarts of Norfolk cricket were so different in their private lives. Their respective experiences in the World Wars may have had something to do with this difference; Michael Falcon served bravely but, through no fault of his own, relatively uneventfully in the Army and was rushed back from the front to be propelled straight into the House of Commons. A lifetime of public service and hard graft lay ahead. Falcon was a true amateur, making not a penny out of cricket (a fact of which his son is very proud) and insisting on making his living outside the game. He was also happily married to Kathleen until he died. In contrast, Bill Edrich was a bomber pilot in the Royal Air Force, flying daredevil raids over Germany and facing death on a regular basis. Like many airmen, he responded by learning to live for the moment, enjoying the consumption of alcohol and the company of women (no fewer than five of whom he married). Although war heroes were granted a certain leeway, Bill's party habits reputedly cost him a place on the 1950/51 Ashes tour. Ralph Barker, in *The Cricketing Family Edrich*, refutes the popularly held view that it was the captain-to-be Freddie Brown who vetoed Edrich's selection and it remains unclear to this day who was responsible for his omission.[69] It must be stressed however that, although he may have been a hard drinker, Edrich was no buffoon like Tennyson and, once on the field of play, his captaincy, as described above, was sharp and incisive.[70]

Minor Counties cricket is, however, an arcane subject, cared for or known about few outside the relevant county boundaries. It is woefully neglected by the media, with BBC Radio Norfolk being one of the few honourable exceptions. Norfolk, geographically isolated from first-class county cricket, still attracts crowds of several hundred to its annual cricket festival (which dates back to 1881) and used to draw thousands, especially against touring teams whose regular visits to Lakenham have been described.[71] Unfortunately support in other counties is less strong and attendances for other Minor Counties games are smaller than those seen in Norfolk.

As a result of this general ignorance of Minor County cricket, Michael Falcon is likely to fade from view, despite his great deeds and the affection with which he is generally held. However, he will

---

69   Whoever did vote against Bill might have regretted their decision in retrospect, for the first two Tests were close-run affairs and Bill's courageous batting might have made all the difference to the destination of the Ashes.

70   Another airman who responded to the experience of facing death on a daily basis by adopting a high-spirited lifestyle was Edrich's drinking chum and Ashes foe Keith Miller. With Bradman as the *de facto* selector-in-chief, Miller's place in the Australian Test team was generally safe because of his ability to bowl bouncers at English Test batsmen, but many think that Miller's lifestyle may have cost him the captaincy when Lindsay Hassett retired.

71   Spectators at Lakenham have been rewarded for their presence by seeing some of the finest cricketers in history make the journey to Norfolk. For instance, Ranjitsinhji, W.G.Grace, Jack Hobbs, C.K.Nayudu and George Headley have all appeared against the county side, whilst great players such as Herbie Taylor, Garry Sobers and Sunil Gavaskar visited Lakenham when it played host to fixtures arranged under the auspices of the Minor Counties. In more recent times, an exhibition match saw a Norfolk team strengthened by a couple of 'given men' defeat a 'Rest of the World' side including stars such as Richie Richardson, Alvin Kallicharan and Javed Miandad but, while games such as may be enjoyable, they are not economically viable in the modern climate.

be remembered for his bowling at Eastbourne in 1921, if nothing else. Oddly enough, even there errors are creeping into the literature about his deeds; one Australian source describes the then 33-year-old as 'a young swing bowler' whilst another gets it horribly wrong, stating that '21-year-old Falcon would renounce first-class cricket in favour of a House of Commons seat'. Let us give the last words on Michael Falcon to the *Eastern Daily Press* and to his team-mate at Eastbourne, Sir Hubert Ashton.

The *Eastern Daily Press*, in a leader headed 'Corinthian' stated: 'Michael Falcon provided his own shining page in the history of this golden game. His public attributes were manifold ... . In cricketing terms it is difficult to say more than that he was Norfolk, playing it and caring for it for more than 70 years ... . He was perhaps our last link with cricket's golden age of the Corinthian amateur. Certainly we shall never see his like again.'

Sir Hubert, also a Conservative MP, wrote in *The Cricketer*: 'Michael Falcon, who died on February 27, aged 87, was one of a long line of Michael Falcons and no doubt the most famous of them all as he was distinguished and outstanding in so many fields: a great public administrator, a devoted servant of the county of Norfolk,

A curiosity.
This undertaker in City Road, Norwich, occupies premises named after Michael Falcon. A modest building not particularly worthy of the great cricketer, but perhaps better than no tribute at all.

and a non-pareil as a father and a family man. Yet in the short space available to us here we must devote ourselves to his achievements as a cricketer: these were many, varied and far-flung but confined initially by the First World War and then by his many public duties. Mike was a well-built, handsome man – a falcon indeed as he ran smoothly to the crease to bowl his distinctly quick stuff. A splendid field and a very adequate bat, he played a great part in that famous match when a team captained by Archie MacLaren beat for the first time that great Australian side of 1921 captained by Warwick Armstrong at Eastbourne in August. It must be remembered that our other fast bowler, Walter Brearley, who had been training for the match for weeks, strained a muscle while batting in the first innings and took no further part in the match. Thus a special burden fell upon Mike, who bore it with his usual debonair but quiet and determined spirit as these figures will for ever testify: 18.4-2-67-6 and 18-2-82-2. His 'victims' included Collins, Macartney, Pellew, Ryder and Armstrong himself. As on this Ash Wednesday we enter another period of Lent at a time when some of us – both old and young – may be rather bewildered by this complicated world, perhaps all of us may for a moment be united and feel comforted by the thought that we thank God for every remembrance of Mike Falcon.'

This bench, at the Norfolk ground at Horsford, recognises Michael Falcon's sixty years of service to Norfolk cricket.

Acknowledgements

Many thanks are due to Tony Webb, for the original suggestion that Michael Falcon would be a suitable subject for the 'Lives in Cricket' series and for supplying me with much material on Falcon. His encouragement, as I made my first foray into authorship outside the field of scientific research, was much appreciated. Peter Wynne-Thomas was an invaluable source of information and very helpful in allowing me access to his unpublished index to *The Cricketer* and hosting me whilst I chased up the references in the Trent Bridge library's run of that magazine.

Amazingly, given that Michael Falcon was born over 120 years ago, four of his five children are still alive. His son, Michael Gascoigne Falcon, has provided me with much material, including many interesting anecdotes which do not survive anywhere else. His sisters, Anne and especially Sybil, have also written of their memories of their father. Michael Gascoigne and Sybil have also been very kind in handing over to my safekeeping many of the photographs that contribute to this volume.

Memories of Michael Falcon have also been kindly provided by Alf Mace, one of only two cricketers still alive who played Minor Counties Championship cricket under Falcon's leadership, whilst stories of Falcon in his extreme old age were provided by Peter Harrison, who was his neighbour in the Cathedral Close in Norwich.

Thanks are due to the staff at the following institutions in Norwich: the Library at the Forum, the Norfolk Record Office (where the relevant Norfolk scorebooks are kept under references SO14/1 and SO14/2) and the Royal Norfolk Regimental Museum. Further afield, invaluable help has come from Rita Boswell at the Harrow School archive; Jayne Ringrose at Pembroke College, Cambridge; Neil Robinson at the MCC Library at Lord's; and from staff at the British Newspaper Library at Colindale; the Guildhall Library in the City of London; the Parliamentary Archive; the National Archive at Kew; and the Cambridge Union Society. Whilst I was researching in London, Rachel Neaman and Tomi Pauk were kind enough to offer me unlimited board and lodging. Roger Mann, Phil Scott and Philip Yaxley have all contributed illustrations from their collections. Philip Scott took a number of photographs specially for this book and Philip Yaxley was kind enough to permit me to cherry-pick from his unique archive of photographs on Norfolk cricket.

Help has also been forthcoming from individuals who share my interest in Norfolk cricket. Reading David Armstrong's history of the county club has given me an invaluable framework around which I could base the structure my life of Falcon: he also pointed me in the direction of Falcon's son and has also provided some important pictures. Mike Davage kindly read a few draft chapters and has since been invaluable in providing first names for many cricketers where once I only had initials; he also managed to obtain Alf Mace's address and some details of Falcon's family. Andy Archer and Frank Devaney have been kind enough to supply some 'colour' on David Walker and Harold Watson respectively.

Various members of the Association of Cricket Statisticians and Historians have been extremely helpful in the production of this 'life' of Michael Falcon. David Jeater has been an excellent, well-informed editor, suggesting many amendments which invariably improved my narrative and correcting my grammar where necessary. David Kelly and David Pracy must be thanked for proof-reading the manuscript. Philip Bailey has speedily answered statistical questions. Zahra Ridge has designed the cover and Pete Griffiths has attended to the time-consuming detail of typesetting and managed the production process. My thanks too, to the Association itself, for assisting with some of the expense of researching Michael Falcon's remarkable life.

Norwich
February, 2010

Bibliography

Books and Articles

John Arlott (ed), *Cricket: The Great Captains*, Pelham, 1971

David Armstrong, *A Short History of Norfolk County Cricket*, The Larks Press, 1990

Philip Bailey (ed), *First–Class Cricket Matches: 1908* (and other years to 1920), ACS Publications, 2005 (and later years)

Philip Bailey, Philip Thorn and Peter Wynne-Thomas, *Who's Who of Cricketers* (Revised Edition), Hamlyn in association with ACS, 1993

Jack Bannister, *A History Of Warwickshire C.C.C.*, Christopher Helm, 1990

Ralph Barker, *The Cricketing Family Edrich*, Pelham, 1976

C.J.Bartlett, 'First-Class Cricketers and Parliament' in *Journal of the Cricket Society, Vol 5(3)*, 1971, pp 66-68

Robert Blake, *Esto Perpetua: Norwich Union Life Insurance Society 1808–1958*, Newman Neame, 1958

Richard Bond, Kenneth Penn and Andrew Rogerson, *Norfolk Origins 4: The North Folk: Angles, Saxons and Danes*, Poppyland Publications, 1990

Lawrence Booth, *Cricket, Lovely Cricket*, Yellow Jersey Press, 2008

Mihir Bose, *Keith Miller: A Cricketing Biography*, George Allen and Unwin, 1980

Gerald Brodribb, *Maurice Tate*, London Magazine Editions, 1976

Gerald Brodribb, *The Croucher: A Biography of Gilbert Jessop*, Constable and Co, 1985

Robert Brooke and Peter Matthews, *Guinness Cricket Firsts*, Guinness Publishing, 1988

Freddie Brown, *Cricket Musketeer*, Nicholas Kaye, 1954

S.Canynge Caple, *The Ashes At Stake*, Worcester Press, 1961

Frank Chester, *How's That!*, Hutchinson, 1956

George Chesterton and Hubert Doggart, *Oxford and Cambridge Cricket*, Willow Books, 1989

R.Rainbird Clarke, *East Anglia*, S.R.Publishers, 1971

Derek Clifford and Timothy Clifford, *John Crome*, Faber and Faber, 1968

Philip Collins and Michael Falcon, *Incogniti Cricket Club: An Account of the American Tour, 1913*, T.W.Thornton, 1914

Denis Compton and Bill Edrich, *Cricket and All That*, Pelham, 1978

Bernard Darwin, *Eton v Harrow at Lord's*, Williams and Norgate, 1926

Michael Down, *Archie: A Biography of A.C.MacLaren*, George Allen and Unwin, 1981

Leslie Duckworth, *S.F.Barnes: Master Bowler*, Hutchinson, 1967

Bill Edrich, *Cricket Heritage*, Stanley Paul, 1947

Bill Edrich, *Cricketing Days*, Stanley Paul, 1950

Alan Edwards, *Lionel Tennyson: Regency Buck*, Robson, 2001

Colin Evans, *Mods and Blockers*, Max Books, 2009

R.Welldon Finn, *Domesday Studies: The Eastern Counties*, Longmans, 1967

Lt-Col Hon Gerald French, *The Corner Stone of English Cricket*, Hutchinson, 1948

Bill Frindall, *The Wisden Book of Test Cricket: 1877–1984*, Queen Anne Press, 1985

David Frith, *Pageant of Cricket*, MacMillan, 1987

David Frith, *Bodyline Autopsy*, Aurum Press, 2002

Alan Gibson, *The Cricket Captains of England*, Cassell, 1979

W.J.Goode, *East Anglian Round Towers and their Churches*, Friends of The Round Tower Churches Society, 1982

Sir Home Gordon, *Background of Cricket*, Arthur Barker, 1939

Edward Grayson, *Corinthians and Cricketers*, Naldrett Press, 1955

Barbara Green and Rachel M.R.Young, *Norwich: The Growth of a City*, Witley Press, 1981

Benny Green (ed), *Wisden Book of Obituaries*, Queen Anne Press, 1986

Peter Griffiths and Peter Wynne-Thomas, *Complete First–Class Match List, Volume I: 1801–1914*, ACS Publications, 1996

Gideon Haigh, *The Big Ship: Warwick Armstrong and the Making of Modern Cricket*, Aurum Press, 2002

Gideon Haigh (ed), *The Penguin Book Of Ashes Anecdote*s: 1882-2005, Penguin Books, 2006

Andrew Hignell, *100 First–Class Umpires,* Tempus Publishing, 2003

Alan Hill, *Bill Edrich: A Biography*, Andre Deutsch, 1994

Geoffrey Holme (ed), *The Norwich School*, The Studio Ltd, 1920

Garrie Hutchinson & John Ross (eds), *200 Seasons of Australian Cricket*, MacMillan, 1997

Gilbert Jessop, *A Cricketer's Log*, Hodder and Stoughton,1922

Jim Ledbetter (ed), *First–Class Cricket: A Complete Record, 1926* (and other years to 1936), ACS Publications, 2009 (and earlier years)

David Lemmon, *Johnny Won't Hit Today*, George Allen & Unwin, 1983

David Lemmon, *Percy Chapman: A Biography*, Queen Anne Press, 1985

David Lemmon and Douglas Smith, *Votes For Cricket*, Breedon Books, 2000

John A.Lester, *A Century of Philadelphia Cricket*, University of Philadelphia Press, 1951

W.R.Lyon, *The Elevens of Three Great Schools: 1805–1929*, Spottiswoode, Ballantyne and Co, 1930

Jeremy Malies, *Great Characters from Cricket's Golden Age*, Robson Books, 2000

Ashley Mallett, *Lords' Dreaming*, Souvenir Press, 2002

Jonathan Mantle, *Norwich Union: The First 200 Years*, James and James, 1997

Christopher Martin-Jenkins, *The Complete Who's Who of Test Cricketers*, Queen Anne Press, 1987

Ronald Mason, *Warwick Armstrong's Australians*, Epworth Press, 1971

Frank Meeres, *A History of Norwich*, Phillimore and Co Ltd, 1998

Douglas Miller, *A History of Bucks County Cricket Club*, ACS Publications, 2006

Patrick Morrah, *Alfred Mynn and the Cricketers of his Time*, Eyre and Spottiswoode, 1963

Oliver Morton, *Eating The Sun*, Fourth Estate, 2007

A.G.Moyes, *Australian Cricket: A History*, Angus and Robertson, 1959

Colin R.Munford, *A Century of Minor Counties Cricket*, Suffolk County Cricket Association, 2004

M.A.Noble, *Gilligan's Men*, Chapman and Hall, 1925

Ian Peebles, *Patsy Hendren: The Cricketer and His Times*, Macmillan and Co, 1969

Roland Perry, *Keith Miller: The Life of a Great All-rounder*, Aurum Press, 2006

Roy Peskett (ed), *The Best Of Cricket: An Anthology*, Newnes, 1982

W.T.Pike (ed), Norfolk and Suffolk, in *East Anglia: Contemporary Biographies*, W.T.Pike, 1911

Carole Rawcliffe and Richard Wilson (eds), *Medieval Norwich*, Continuum International Publishing, 2006

P.H.Reaney and R.M.Wilson, *A Dictionary of English Surnames* (Third Edition), Oxford University Press, 1997

Fred Root, *A Cricket Pro's Lot*, Edward Arnold and Co, 1937

Rowland Ryder, *Cricket Calling*, Faber and Faber, 1995

Derek Salberg, *Much Ado About Cricket*, K.A.F.Brewin Books, 1987

E.H.D.Sewell, *Cricket Points*, The Sporting Life, 1911

E.H.D.Sewell, *Who's Won The Toss?*, Stanley Paul, 1943

E.H.D.Sewell, *Overthrows*, Stanley Paul, 1946

Michael Stenton and Stephen Lees, *Who's Who of British Members of Parliament, Volume III: 1919–1945*, Harvester Press, 1979

E.W.Swanton, *As I Said at the Time*, William Collins, 1983

E.W.Swanton, *Gubby Allen: Man of Cricket*, Hutchinson/Stanley Paul, 1985

E.W.Swanton and John Woodcock (eds), *Barclays World Of Cricket*, Collins, 1986

Geoff Tibballs, *Cricket's Greatest Characters*, J.R.Books, 2008

[Sir] Pelham Warner, *My Cricketing Life*, Hodder and Stoughton, 1921

[Sir] Pelham Warner, *The Book of Cricket*, J.M. Dent and Sons, 1922

Sir Pelham Warner, *Lord's: 1787–1945*, Harrap, 1946

Sir Pelham Warner, *Cricket Between Two Wars*, Sporting Handbooks, 1946

Sir Pelham Warner, *Gentlemen v Players: 1806–1949*, George G.Harrap, 1950

Sir Pelham Warner, *Long Innings*, Harrap, 1951

Tony Webb (ed), *The Minor Counties Championship: 1895* (and other years to 1903), ACS Publications, 2004 (and later years)

E.M.Wellings, *Vintage Cricketers*, George Allen and Unwin, 1983

Wilfrid S.White, *Sydney Barnes*, E.F.Hudson Ltd, 1937

William White, *History, Gazetteer and Directory of Norfolk* (Fourth Edition). Spottiswoode and Co, 1883

Tom Williamson, *The Origins of Norfolk*, Manchester University Press, 1993

Peter Wynne-Thomas, *The Complete History of Cricket Tours at Home and Abroad*, Hamlyn, 1989

Philip Yaxley, *Looking Back at Norfolk Cricket*, Nostalgia Publications, 1997

In addition to these specific publications, I have made use of books in the ACS *'Famous Cricketers'* series and earlier issues in the *'Lives in Cricket'* series.

Newspapers and Periodicals

Cricket magazine

The Cricketer magazine

Crickinia annual

The Daily Telegraph newspaper

Eastern Daily Press newspaper

Eastern Evening News newspaper

Hansard, House of Commons Official Reports

The Harrovian magazine

Manchester Guardian newspaper

Minor Counties Handbooks

Morning Post newspaper

The Norfolk Chronicle and Norwich Gazette newspaper

Norfolk County Cricket Club Handbooks

Norfolk News and Weekly Press newspaper

Norfolk Weekly Standard and Argus newspaper

Norwich Mercury (and *People's Weekly Journal*) newspaper

The Times newspaper

Westminster Gazette newspaper

Wisden Cricketers' Almanack annual

Websites

www.ancestry.co.uk

www.cricketarchive.com

www.cricket-online.org

www.hansard.millbanksystems.com

www.nationaltrust.org

Appendix:
Some Statistics

First-Class Cricket: Batting and Fielding

	M	I	NO	R	HS	Ave	100	50	Ct
1908	10	19	1	544	122	30.22	1	1	9
1909	6	12	0	383	130	31.92	1	-	2
1910	10	17	0	369	96	21.71	-	2	8
1911	13	23	1	831	134	37.77	2	3	7
1912	5	10	2	107	36	13.37	-	-	5
1913	4	8	3	49	18*	9.80	-	-	4
1914	2	4	0	66	27	16.50	-	-	1
1919	7	11	3	66	14	8.25	-	-	1
1920	4	8	1	83	27*	11.86	-	-	1
1921	2	4	1	105	77*	35.00	-	1	-
1922	1	2	0	52	43	26.00	-	-	-
1923	3	5	0	86	28	17.20	-	-	-
1924	3	6	3	76	34*	25.33	-	-	1
1925	1	2	0	95	77	47.50	-	1	-
1926	4	6	4	142	86*	71.00	-	1	1
1927	3	5	1	40	16	10.00	-	-	2
1928	1	1	0	3	3	3.00	-	-	1
1929	2	3	0	39	27	13.00	-	-	-
1930	1	1	0	5	5	5.00	-	-	-
1931	2	2	0	19	12	9.50	-	-	1
1932	1	2	2	34	19*	-	-	-	-
1933	1	1	1	30	30*	-	-	-	-
1934	1	1	1	5	5*	-	-	-	-
1935	1	1	0	37	37	37.00	-	-	-
1936	1	1	1	16	16*	-	-	-	-
Career	**89**	**155**	**25**	**3282**	**134**	**25.25**	**4**	**9**	**44**

Notes: Falcon was dismissed caught 71 times (54.6%); bowled 40 times (30.8%); lbw 16 times (12.3%) and run out three times (2.3%). He was never stumped, nor did he ever hit his wicket. His percentage of dismissals lbw is not high by modern standards, but is high for a player who played much of his cricket before the Great War. The bowler who took his wicket most often was Bill Hitch, four times: eight bowlers dismissed him three times.

First-Class Cricket: Bowling

	O	M	R	W	BB	Ave	5i	10m
1908	24	4	116	4	1-5	29.00	-	-
1909	11	1	57	2	2-50	28.50	-	-
1910	37.1	2	142	3	2-36	47.33	-	-
1911	268.3	46	895	44	5-25	20.34	3	-
1912	89.1	25	237	22	6-37	10.77	3	-
1913	96.2	15	389	14	6-58	27.78	2	-
1914	78.4	15	287	17	7-70	16.88	2	1

1919	173.3	27	587	25	6-41	23.48	2	-
1920	131.3	16	594	25	6-62	23.76	3	-
1921	75.3	8	359	12	6-67	29.92	1	-
1922	26	4	107	4	4-107	26.75	-	-
1923	106	17	365	13	6-76	28.07	1	-
1924	109	15	404	17	7-78	23.76	2	-
1925	19.2	3	78	5	5-65	15.60	1	-
1926	100	17	323	4	3-124	80.75	-	-
1927	62	3	239	6	4-60	39.83	-	-
1928	24	4	66	4	4-45	16.50	-	-
1929	39	7	101	2	2-42	50.50	-	-
1930	24	4	77	1	1-52	77.00	-	-
1931	44.2	12	137	5	4-54	27.40	-	-
1932	28	12	40	0	-	-	-	-
1933	6	2	25	0	-	-	-	-
1934	8	0	58	1	1-43	58.00	-	-
1935	6	1	28	1	1-7	28.00	-	-
1936	3	0	16	0	-	-	-	-
Career	**1590**	**260**	**5727**	**231**	**7-70**	**24.79**	**20**	**1**

Notes: Throughout Falcon's first-class career, overs were of six balls. He conceded, on average, 3.60 runs per over – an expensive rate for a front-line bowler – and took wickets at a rate of one per 41.30 balls. He took 127 wickets caught (55.0%), of which five (2.2%) were caught and bowled; 93 wickets bowled (40.3%); ten wickets lbw (4.3%), and one wicket stumped (0.4%). Of his ten lbw victims, five were taken after 1926 when he had ceased to be a strike bowler. Before 1927 Falcon took 211 wickets including only five lbws at a percentage of only 2.4 – this is a very low figure for a 'serious' bowler, even allowing for the fact that lbws were rarer at the time. The batsmen whom he dismissed most frequently were Jack Hobbs (six times), and David Denton, Wilfred Rhodes and George Wood, all five times.

First-Class Cricket: Innings of Fifty or More (13)

Score	For	Opponent	Venue	Season
60	Cambridge Univ[1]	Sussex	Fenner's	1908
122	Cambridge Univ[2]	MCC	Lord's	1908
130	Cambridge Univ[2]	Sussex	Hove	1909
63	Cambridge Univ[1]	Yorkshire	Fenner's	1910
96	Cambridge Univ[2]	Gentlemen of England	Eastbourne	1910
134	Cambridge Univ[2]	Sussex	Fenner's	1911
115	MCC[1]	Leicestershire	Lord's	1911
70*	Cambridge Univ[2]	Surrey	The Oval	1911
65	Cambridge Univ[1]	MCC	Lord's	1911
75	Gentlemen[1]	Players	Scarborough	1911
77*	Free Foresters[2]	Oxford University	The Parks	1921
77	Free Foresters[2]	Cambridge University	Fenner's	1925
86*	Free Foresters[2]	Cambridge University	Fenner's	1926

Note: The index figures [1] and [2] in this and the tables below indicate the innings in which the feat was achieved.

First-Class Cricket: Five Wickets or More in an Innings (20)

Analysis	For	Opponent	Venue	Season
20.4-6-50-5	Cambridge University	Indians[2]	Fenner's	1911
16-5-40-5	Cambridge University	Sussex[2]	Hove	1911
15.3-6-25-5	Cambridge University	MCC[2]	Lord's	1911
16-5-37-6	Free Foresters	Cambridge Univ[2]	Fenner's	1912
10.1-4-16-5	MCC	Yorkshire[1]	Scarborough	1912
18-5-47-6	L.Robinson's XI	South Africans[1]	Old Buckenham	1912
15-3-55-5	L.Robinson's XI	Cambridge Univ[1]	Old Buckenham	1913
14.2-2-58-6	Gentlemen	Players[1]	The Oval	1913
18-4-41-6	Free Foresters	Cambridge Univ[1]	Fenner's	1914
22.4-9-70-7	Free Foresters	Cambridge Univ[2]	Fenner's	1914
25-5-67-5	P.F.Warner's XI	Oxford University[1]	The Parks	1919
14-3-41-6	Gentlemen of England	AIF[1]	Lord's	1919
28-4-88-5	Free Foresters	Oxford University[1]	The Parks	1920
15-4-62-6	Free Foresters	Cambridge Univ[1]	Fenner's	1920
26.5-2-157-5	Gentlemen	Players[1]	The Oval	1920
18.4-2-67-6	England XI	Australians[1]	Eastbourne	1921
31-5-76-6	Free Foresters	Cambridge Univ[1]	Fenner's	1923
17-1-78-7	Gentlemen	Players[1]	The Oval	1924
34-6-103-5	Minor Counties	South Africans[2]	Lakenham	1924
15.2-2-65-5	Free Foresters	Cambridge Univ[1]	Fenner's	1925

Note: Falcon took ten or more wickets in a match once, for Free Foresters v Cambridge University at Fenner's in 1914. His returns were 18-4-41-6 and 22.4-9-70-7, giving match totals of 40.4-13-111-13.

The four tables below give details of Falcon's performances in Minor Counties cricket for Norfolk. The matches covered include all the Minor Counties Championship games in which he made appearances, plus certain other matches where Norfolk fielded a full first eleven in two-day fixtures against high-quality opposition. The opponents in these matches include MCC, first-class touring sides, Free Foresters, Suffolk, Lionel Robinson's XI, Eton Ramblers and Harrow Wanderers.

Minor Counties Cricket: Batting and Fielding

	M	I	NO	R	HS	Ave	100	50	Ct	Pos
1906	1	2	0	5	5	2.50	-	-	-	n/a
1907	4	7	1	458	112	76.33	3	1	2	1
1908	6	10	0	147	54	14.70	-	1	1	10
1910	9	13	0	315	56	24.23	-	3	11	6
1911	9	18	2	631	114	39.44	2	4	3	3
1912	9	16	3	538	143	41.38	1	3	4	1
1913	7	11	0	410	155	37.27	1	1	1	1
1914	7	11	1	332	93	33.20	-	1	2	3
1919	1	2	0	38	33	19.00	-	-	-	n/a
1920	6	9	1	480	205	60.00	2	1	7	1
1921	9	14	1	401	111	30.85	2	1	5	1
1922	14	22	1	728	113	34.67	1	4	12	3
1923	11	20	2	678	98	37.67	-	6	5	2
1924	8	12	2	580	148	58.00	2	2	6	1

Year										
1925	10	15	1	425	136	30.36	1	-	6	4
1926	9	16	2	672	107*	48.00	1	6	1	1
1927	10	14	1	518	150	39.85	2	2	3	1
1928	11	19	3	692	115	43.25	2	3	4	1
1929	11	20	1	658	189	34.63	1	4	2	1
1930	8	13	1	289	120	24.08	1	1	1	2
1931	10	16	2	258	47	18.43	-	-	8	4
1932	11	19	2	345	64*	20.29	-	2	8	3
1933	13	18	1	420	70	24.71	-	2	4	9
1934	10	13	1	233	54	19.42	-	1	2	9
1935	11	16	3	397	67*	30.54	-	2	8	4
1936	10	10	2	185	65	23.12	-	1	1	8
1937	13	19	0	479	72	25.21	-	4	4	8
1938	11	16	1	273	62	18.20	-	3	3	11
1939	13	15	3	552	79	46.00	-	6	4	3
1946	5	8	2	178	70*	29.67	-	1	2	1
Career	**267**	**414**	**40**	**12315**	**205**	**32.93**	**22**	**66**	**120**	

Notes: Falcon did not play in Minor Counties cricket in 1909. He was caught 187 times (50.0%); bowled 115 times (30.7%); lbw 59 times (15.8%); stumped three times (0.8%) and run out ten times (2.7%). These percentages are similar to those of his first-class career. He was never stumped in the first-class arena and rarely so dismissed in the Minor Counties game: he never hit his wicket. The right-hand column gives Falcon's position in the Norfolk averages for each season. He finished top of these in 11 seasons (ranging from 1907 to 1946) and in the top four in a further ten seasons: for 17 consecutive seasons (1911-1932) he featured in the top four.

Minor Counties Cricket: Bowling

	O	M	R	W	BB	Ave	5i	10m	Pos
1906	5	0	18	0	-	-	-	-	n/a
1907	14	2	63	1	1-62	63.00	-	-	n/a
1908	35.5	4	145	2	1-6	72.50	-	-	n/a
1910	228.5	63	689	39	7-53	17.67	2	1	4
1911	146.3	32	489	22	5-51	22.23	2	-	2
1912	194.5	35	581	38	6-46	15.29	3	-	5
1913	167.3	35	518	36	6-18	14.39	5	1	4
1914	173.3	31	568	39	6-16	14.56	3	1	2
1919	21	6	48	4	4-48	12.00	-	-	n/a
1920	170	42	393	46	7-49	8.54	6	2	1
1921	234.2	40	740	53	6-42	13.96	5	1	2
1922	297	72	889	72	7-37	12.35	6	1	2
1923	295.5	67	846	54	8-41	15.67	3	1	2
1924	256	46	686	45	7-57	15.24	4	1	3
1925	254	46	696	37	6-33	18.81	3	-	4
1926	235.4	54	716	37	5-41	19.35	4	-	1
1927	192	35	544	28	5-57	19.42	1	-	4
1928	228	49	648	43	7-40	15.07	4	1	2
1929	196.2	37	649	29	6-39	22.38	2	-	4
1930	109.3	27	268	13	6-24	20.61	1	-	6
1931	118.1	25	308	20	6-39	15.40	1	-	4
1932	88.4	23	217	7	2-34	31.00	-	-	7
1933	100.2	25	205	12	2-12	17.08	-	-	4
1934	59.4	14	155	4	2-20	38.75	-	-	n/a
1935	104	24	270	9	4-44	30.00	-	-	6
1936	95	31	194	17	4-46	11.41	-	-	2
1937	146.1	36	434	20	5-49	21.70	1	-	4

1938	101.4	29	252	10	4-34	25.20	-	-	4
1939	15.6	3	59	2	1-12	29.50	-	-	n/a
1946	did not bowl								
Career	**(6b) 4269.2**	**930**	**12288**	**739**	**8-41**	**16.63**	**56**	**10**	
	(8b) 15.6	**3**							

Notes: Overs were of eight balls in 1939 and of six in all other seasons. Falcon conceded, on average, 2.86 runs per six-ball over – compared with 3.60 runs per over in the first-class game. He took wickets at the rate of one per 34.83 balls – rather more frequently than his first-class figures. He took 358 wickets caught (48.4%), of which 28 (3.8%) were caught and bowled; 305 wickets bowled (41.3%); 62 wickets lbw (8.4%); 12 wickets stumped (1.6%) and two wickets hit wicket (0.3%). Ten of the stumpings came after Falcon ceased to be a genuine pace bowler, but two came in 1914 and 1922 (both by Guy Pedder) when he was still speedy. The right-hand column gives Falcon's position in the Norfolk averages for each season. He finished top of these in two seasons and in the top four in a further 17 seasons: for 12 consecutive seasons (1913 to 1929) he featured in the top four.

Minor Counties Cricket: Centuries (22)

Score	Opponent	Venue	Season
110	Bedfordshire[1]	Lakenham	1907
112	Cambridgeshire[1]	Fenner's	1907
102*	Harrow Wanderers[2]	Lakenham	1907
114	Cambridgeshire[1]	Fenner's	1911
104	Suffolk[2]	Lakenham	1911
143	Hertfordshire[2]	Lakenham	1912
155	Bedfordshire[1]	Lakenham	1913
134	Essex Second XI[1]	Witham	1920
205	Hertfordshire[1]	Cheshunt	1920
107	Cambridgeshire[1]	Lakenham	1921
111	Bedfordshire[1]	Lakenham	1921
113	Staffordshire[1]	Lakenham	1922
148	Surrey Second XI[1]	Hunstanton	1924
129*	Staffordshire[2]	Lakenham	1924
136	Leicestershire Second XI[1]	Leicester	1925
107*	Kent Second XI[2]	Chatham	1926
150	Hertfordshire[1]	Cokenach	1927
114	Kent Second XI[2]	Lakenham	1927
115	Surrey Second XI[1]	The Oval	1928
104	Buckinghamshire[1]	Ascott Park	1928
189	Leicestershire Second XI[1]	Hinckley	1929
120	Surrey Second XI[1]	The Oval	1930

Minor Counties Cricket: Five Wickets or More in an Innings (56)

Analysis	Opponent	Venue	Season
19-7-53-7	Nottinghamshire Second XI[1]	Lakenham	1910
18-4-57-5	Bedfordshire[1]	Lakenham	1910
20.3-6-71-5	Hertfordshire[1]	St Albans	1911
15-6-51-5	Bedfordshire[2]	Lakenham	1911
17.1-3-46-6	Hertfordshire[1]	Lakenham	1912
8.2-1-19-5	Suffolk[2]	Lakenham	1912
9-1-43-5	MCC[2]	Great Yarmouth	1912
12.2-6-18-6	Hertfordshire[1]	Bushey	1913

Analysis	Opponent	Venue	Season
27.4-3-87-6	Staffordshire[1]	Stoke-on-Trent	1913
14-2-51-5	Cambridgeshire[2]	Fenner's	1913
13-3-25-5	Staffordshire[1]	Lakenham	1913
16.3-3-44-5	Staffordshire[2]	Lakenham	1913
25.3-4-83-5	MCC[1]	Lord's	1914
16-5-59-6	Cambridgeshire[1]	Lakenham	1914
7.2-1-16-6	Cambridgeshire[2]	Lakenham	1914
14-2-35-6	Essex Second XI[1]	Witham	1920
24-9-39-5	Bedfordshire[1]	Bedford	1920
23-8-39-5	Bedfordshire[2]	Bedford	1920
15.2-3-30-6	Essex Second XI[2]	Lakenham	1920
18.4-3-49-7	Hertfordshire[1]	Lakenham	1920
12-6-20-5	Bedfordshire[1]	Lakenham	1920
25.3-0-93-5	Staffordshire[1]	Lakenham	1921
20-3-84-6	Staffordshire[1]	Walsall	1921
19-2-63-6	Kent Second XI[1]	Hythe	1921
19-5-56-6	Kent Second XI[2]	Hythe	1921
15.5-2-42-6	Cambridgeshire[1]	Fenner's	1921
14.4-3-46-5	Surrey Second XI[2]	Lakenham	1922
27-9-57-5	Bedfordshire[1]	Lakenham	1922
13-3-38-5	Bedfordshire[1]	Luton	1922
15-3-58-5	Eton Ramblers[1]	Lakenham	1922
16-7-37-7	Eton Ramblers[2]	Lakenham	1922
13.2-5-32-5	Cambridgeshire[2]	King's Lynn	1922
34-8-91-5	Bedfordshire[1]	Luton	1923
34-8-107-5	Hertfordshire[1]	Lakenham	1923
17.1-5-41-8	Bedfordshire[2]	King's Lynn	1923
9-1-24-5	Staffordshire[1]	Old Hill	1924
18-4-37-7	Surrey Second XI[1]	Hunstanton	1924
22-8-38-5	Leicestershire Second XI[2]	Lakenham	1924
29-6-87-5	Staffordshire[1]	Lakenham	1924
15.5-6-33-6	Staffordshire[1]	Lakenham	1925
20-7-29-5	Hertfordshire[1]	Cokenach	1925
13.1-3-25-5	Hertfordshire[1]	Lakenham	1925
23-4-98-5	Leicestershire Second XI[1]	Hinckley	1926
22.1-5-52-5	Kent Second XI[1]	Chatham	1926
23.2-9-41-5	Hertfordshire[1]	Cokenach	1926
25-6-87-5	Surrey Second XI[1]	Lakenham	1926
18-2-57-5	Buckinghamshire[2]	High Wycombe	1927
25.1-3-82-7	Buckinghamshire[1]	Ascott Park	1928
9-3-28-6	Leicestershire Second XI[2]	Lakenham	1928
16-3-40-7	Buckinghamshire[1]	Lakenham	1928
18-6-47-6	Buckinghamshire[2]	Lakenham	1928
11.4-1-50-5	Leicestershire Second XI[1]	Hinckley	1929
12.1-1-39-6	Surrey Second XI[1]	Lakenham	1929
20.3-13-24-6	Buckinghamshire[1]	Ascott Park	1930
15-5-39-6	Kent Second XI[2]	Beckenham	1931
13.4-4-49-5	Cambridgeshire[2]	Hunstanton	1937

Minor Counties Cricket: Ten Wickets or More in a Match (10)

Analysis	Opponent	Venue	Season
30-9-93-10	Nottinghamshire Second XI	Lakenham	1910
29.3-6-69-10	Staffordshire	Lakenham	1913
23.2-6-75-12	Cambridgeshire	Lakenham	1914
47-17-78-10	Bedfordshire	Bedford	1920
33.4-5-105-11	Hertfordshire	Lakenham	1920
38-7-119-12	Kent Second XI	Hythe	1921
31-10-95-12	Eton Ramblers	Lakenham	1922
34.1-7-98-12	Bedfordshire	King's Lynn	1923

38-8-78-11	Surrey Second XI	Hunstanton	1924
34-9-87-13	Buckinghamshire	Lakenham	1928

Note: Of Falcon's ten ten-wicket match returns, no fewer than eight were taken at home: six at Lakenham and one each at King's Lynn and Hunstanton.

Minor Counties Cricket: All-Round Performances

Analysis	Opponent	Venue	Season
56, 7: 4-36, 2-28	Durham	Sunderland	1910
51, -: 7-53, 3-40	Nottinghamshire Second XI	Lakenham	1910
64, 27*: 2-22, 4-56	Northumberland	Lakenham	1911
61, 51*: 0-14, 5-51	Bedfordshire	Lakenham	1911
36, 143: 6-46, 1-43	Hertfordshire	Lakenham	1912
52, -: 2-58, 5-51	Cambridgeshire	Fenner's	1913
23, 93: 4-28, 2-82	Hertfordshire	Lakenham	1914
134, 3*: 6-35, 2-50	Essex Second XI	Witham	1920
74, -: 5-20, 1-9	Bedfordshire	Lakenham	1920
0, 82*: 6-84, 1-12	Staffordshire	Walsall	1921
107, -: 4-13, 4-20	Cambridgeshire	Lakenham	1921
111, -: 3-45, 2-31	Bedfordshire	Lakenham	1921
77, -: 1-10, 5-32	Cambridgeshire	King's Lynn	1922
98, -: 4-54, 4-77	Hertfordshire	Stevenage	1923
50, 66*: 5-91, -	Bedfordshire	Luton	1923
51, 43*: 5-107, -	Hertfordshire	Lakenham	1923
87, 49: 2-46, 3-18	Kent Second XI	Lakenham	1923
148, -: 7-37, 4-41	Surrey Second XI	Hunstanton	1924
98*, 4: 1-53, 5-38	Leicestershire Second XI	Lakenham	1924
19, 129*: 5-87, 1-19	Staffordshire	Lakenham	1924
136, -: 1-41, 4-40	Leicestershire Second XI	Leicester	1925
33, 42: 5-98, -	Leicestershire Second XI	Hinckley	1926
56, 107*: 5-52, 1-18	Kent Second XI	Chatham	1926
83, -: 5-41, -	Hertfordshire	Cokenach	1926
9,114: 3-61, 2-29	Kent Second XI	Lakenham	1927
104, 1: 7-82, -	Buckinghamshire	Ascott Park	1928
3, 98: 0-3, 6-28	Leicestershire Second XI	Lakenham	1928
11, 60: 3-23, 3-79	Buckinghamshire	Ascott Park	1929
189, -: 5-50, 0-31	Leicestershire Second XI	Hinckley	1929

Note: His 1928 performance at Ascott Park was the first time a player had scored a century and taken a hat-trick in the same Minor Counties Championship match.

Sources: cricketarchive.com, *Wisden* Cricketers' Almanacks and Norfolk C.C.C. scorebooks.

Index

A page number in bold type indicates an illustration.

Acle, Norfolk 52, 95, 106
Advisory County Cricket Committee 40
Agriculture and Labour 'party' 44, 45
Alington, Rev C.A. 55
All-Edrich XI 90, 110, 111
All Hallows, Community of,
    Ditchingham, Norfolk 106
All India touring side **85**, 98
Allen, Sir George ('Gubby') 38, 40
Allenby, Field-Marshal Lord 42
Allen Park, Biddenham, Norfolk 59
Ames, L.E.G. 40
Amos, Carl 91
Arkell, Anne (daughter) 94, 97, 101, 103
Arkell, Peter (son-in-law) 97
Armistead Brothers 36
Armstrong, D.J.M. 5, 6, 28, 100, 126,
    127
Armstrong, Rev H.B.J. 5, 6, 41
Armstrong, W.W. 62, 63, 71, 116, 121,
    130
Arnold, E.G. 75
Ascott Park, Wing, Buckinghamshire 80
Ashes tour, 1901/02 116
Ashes tour, 1911/12 119, 120
Ashes tour, 1920/21 39, 62, 120
Ashes tour, 1950/51 128
Ashton, C.T. 62, **64**
Ashton, Gilbert 62, **64**
Ashton, Sir Hubert 60, 62, 63, **64**, 65,
    129, 130
Australia (country) 22, 34, 118
Australian Cricket Board of Control 39
Australian Imperial Forces 58, 59,
    117-119
Australians, touring side 20, 28, 30, 33,
    62, 63, 65, 66, 71, 75, **76**, 77, 78, 80,
    116-118

Baldwin of Bewdley, Rt Hon Lord (British
    Prime Minister) 51
Ballance, T.G.L. 83, 88, 90, 103, 104
Bally, J.H. 81, **81**, 103
Bardsley, Warren 75

Barnes, S.F. 6, 26, 34, 70, 74, 75, 82,
    105, 112, 116, 117, 119, 120, 124,
    125
Barrett, L.A. 111, **111**
Barton, A.W. 103
Barton, M.R. 104
Battelley, B.L. 107
Beadsmoore, W.A. 65, 69, 72, 73, **76**, 79,
    81, 82, 125
Bedford 36
Bedford, Rev W.K.R. 36-37
Bedfordshire C.C.C. 14, 19, 22, 23, 31,
    41, 54, 59, 61, 68
Berkshire C.C.C. 22, 72, 124
Berry, M.J. 123
Bird, M.C. 14
Birkbeck, Christopher 10
Birkbeck, G. W. **23**, **29**, 41
Birley, Sir Oswald 108
Bishop's Stortford College 61
Blake, G.F. 45
Blickling Hall, Norfolk 10
Blofield, Norfolk 44, 49, 90
Blythe, Colin ('Charlie') 75
Bonar Law, Rt Hon Andrew (British
    Prime Minister) 44, 45
Booth, M.W. 120
Bosanquet, B.J.T. 27, 33
Boswell, C.S.R. ('Bozzy') 104, 112
Bracondale School, Norwich 98
Braund, L.C. 24
Brearley, Walter 27, 62, 63, 130
Bretwalda 7
Britannia Barracks, Norwich 95, 103
B.B.C. radio 90
Brooke, Norfolk 51
Brown, F.R. 37, 128
Browne, C.R. 80
Buckinghamshire C.C.C. 65, 66, 79, 80,
    83, 84, **85**, 88, 89, 98, 105, 116, 124
Buller J.S. 86
Burlingham Demonstration Station,
    Norfolk 95
Burrows, Lt-Gen M.B. 62
Burton, F.A. 124, 125
Buxton, D.G. 86, 104

Buxton, E.G. 50, 55

Cadogan Terrace, Chelsea 25
Sir Julien Cahn's XI 89
Cambridge XI, A 58
Cambridge Union Society 43
Cambridge University 15, 17, 26, 43, 62,
   63, 72, 82, 96, 108
Cambridge University C.C. 8, 12, 15, 17,
   18, 19-22, 26, 27, 33, 35-38, 54, 55,
   57, 60, 62, 63, 68, 74-75, 75, 78, 93,
   117, 122
Cambridge University Ladies' C.C. 96
Cambridgeshire C.C.C. 14, 19, 29, 35,
   36, 61, 87, 89, 90, 105
'Carmody' field 36
Carr, A.W. 122
Carter, G.T. 41
Carter, R.D. 66
Carter-Jonas, Louise 16
Cator, John 43, 44, 48, 51-52, 55
Census, 1891 10
Census, 1901 12
Chaplin, H.P. 27
Chapman, A.P.F. 62, **64**, 72, 73
Chatham, Kent 77
Cheshire C.C.C. 124
Christopherson, Stanley 39, **81**
C.E.Y.M.S. C.C., Norwich 90
Clark, John (son-in-law) 97
Clark, Rachel (daughter) 94, 97
Cokenach, Hertfordshire 89
Coldham, J.M. 72, 73, **76**, 83, **85**
Collins, H.L. 118, 119, 130
Colman, A.R. 103
Colman, D.W.J. 103
Colman, G.R.R. **32**, 34, 55, 66, 69, 72,
   73, 75, **76**, 82, 87, 88, 103
Commission on Agriculture 45, 47, 51
Conservative Party ('Unionists') 16,
   43-45, 47, 50-51, 53, 89, 106, 130
Corbett, Sir John (Admiral) 10
County Championship, First-Class 8, 10,
   34, 39, 75, 78, 83, 99, 100, 115, 126
Cowie, A.G. 22
Creber, Harry 35
Cricket magazine 19, 23
The Cricketer magazine 37, 57, 77, 86,
   112, 116-118, 125, 130
Crown Office Row, Temple, London 25
Cumberland 10, 95, **95**
Cunliffe, F.D. 111

Daily Telegraph newspaper 19-21, 27,
   35, 59, 60, 70,71

Daniell, John 120
Davies, G.B. 36
Denton, David 59
Derbyshire C.C.C. 122
Devizes, Wiltshire 54
Devon 16
Devon C.C.C. 124
Ditchingham, Norfolk 106
Doggart, A.G. 72
Domesday Book 7
Douglas, J.W.H.T. 27, **32**, 58, 59, 63, 75,
   117, 119-122
Douglas, C.K. 68
Down's Syndrome 94
Drayton, Norfolk 46
Druce, N.F. 37
Dunkirk, France 16
Durham C.C.C. 72, 84

East Anglia 7, 48
Eastbourne, The Saffrons Ground 62,
   64, 71, 72, 129, 130
East Dereham, Norfolk 28, 33
Eastern Provincial Division, National
   Unionist Assoc. 48
East Norfolk C.C. 90
East Norfolk Unionist/Conservative
   Association 43, 48, 50
The Eastern Daily Press newspaper 14,
   23, 42, 49, 50, 52, 53, 59, 65, 66, 74,
   81, 83, 84, 86-91, 96, 104, 108, 114,
   116, 129
Edrich family 82, 99
Edrich, B.R. 106
Edrich, E.H. 77-78, 83, 89, 104, 106, 110
Edrich, G.A. 5, 83, 101, 103, 104, 106,
   111
Edrich, J.H. 8
Edrich, W.J. 5, 8, 61, 83, 84, **85**, 86, 90,
   91, 93-94, 98-100, 106, 111, **111**,
   123, 125-129
Edwards, Very Rev David (son-in-law) 97
Edwards, Frank 66, 105, 124, 125
Edwards, Sybil (daughter) 79, 94-97,
   101, 106, 112
England XI 30, 63, 64, **64**
England limited-overs XI 10
English Schools' Under-15 eleven 112
Essex 7, 56-58, 92-94
Essex C.C.C. 59
Essex C.C.C. Second XI 15, 59
Essex Court, Temple, London 45, **45**
Eton College 55, 87
Eton College eleven 12, 14, 15
Eton Ramblers C.C. 67

Fakenham and District 58
Falcon, Andrew (grandson) 97
Falcon, Claire (granddaughter) 97
Falcon, Greta (sister-in-law) 15
Falcon, Isabella (sister) 10, 16
Falcon, Joseph Henry ('Harry') (brother)
    10, 15, 41, 42, 47
Falcon, Mary (daughter) 94, 98

Falcon, Michael
  all-rounder in Minor Counties cricket
    82, 123-126
  amateur status 125, 127, 129
  ancestry and birth 10, **11**
  article on spin bowling in *The
    Cricketer* magazine 112
  Ashes tour of 1924/25 118
  barrister in London 25, **25**, 45, **45**
  batting 5, 19, 20,, 21, 27, 28, 36, 59,
    63, 65, 71, 81-83, 86, 91, 92, **92**
  batting achievements:
    for Cambridge U *v* M.C.C., 1908 19
    for Cambridge U *v* Sussex, 1911 26
    for Norfolk *v* Hertfordshire, 1920 59
    Norfolk v Hertfordshire, 1946 105
  'behind the scenes' work for Norfolk
    cricket 5, 57, 60, 69-70, 89-91, 93,
    108, 113, 126
  'bodyline' sub-Committee 39, 40
  bowling 23, 30, 31, 34-36, 58-60, 63,
    65, 68, 70-75, 77, 79, 80, 83, 84, 89,
    90, 109, 119
  bowling achievements:
    for Cambridge U *v* Indians, 1911 26
    for L.Robinson's XI *v* South Africans,
      1912 31
    for Incogniti *v* Philadelphia, 1913
      33, 34
    for Free Foresters *v* Cambridge U,
      1914 36
    for Gentlemen *v* A.I.F., 1919 58, 59,
      117-119
    for MacLaren's side *v* Australians,
      1921 62-65, **64**, 71, 72, 117, 129,
      130
    for Minor Counties North *v* South,
      1925 74
    for Minor Counties *v* Australians,
      1926 75, **76**, 77
  captain of Cambridge University 21,
    22, 26
  possible captain of England 120, 121
  captain of Minor Counties side, 1924
    71-73, **72**, 117-118

captain of Norfolk 8, 23-26, 28, 31, 49,
    76, **81**, 82, 84, **85**, 86-88, 90, 91, 99,
    104, 106, 120, 121, 126-127
Challenge match defeat, 1922 66
character 50, 53, 96, 97, 101, 112, 114
children's achievements 96-98
clustering of wickets in first-class
    games 74
Conservative Party chairman at
    Yarmouth 89, 103, 106
death and funeral service 113, 114
director of Norwich Union and Lacon
    brewery 92, 93, 102, 108, **108**, 109,
    113
encouragement of Bill Edrich 83, 94,
    98-100
general elections of 1918 to 1923
    42-54, 56, 69, 89
emergence as a bowler 13, 22, 23, 26,
    27
family life at North Burlingham 40,
    83, 93-97, **94**, **95**, 101, 103, 112
fielding 23, 126
first player to score century and take
    hat-trick in a Minor Counties game
    143
Falcon Cup competition 69
friendship with Frank Mann 20, 25,
    39, 94
life at Havering-atte-Bower, Essex 56,
    57, 57, 92
High Sheriff of Norfolk 102, **102**
Home Guard service 101, **102**, 103
hop merchant 56, 92
long-serving captain of Norfolk 8, 10,
    123
loyalty to Norfolk 8, 9, 26, 36, 115,
    116, 119, 121, 123, 126
Alf Mace's recollections 106, 107
makes initial impression as a batsman
    12-15, **13**, 17, 19, 20
M.C.C. Committee membership 38-40,
    87
marrying Kathleen Gascoigne 54, 55
Member of Parliament for East Norfolk
    46-51
Middlesex qualification 26, 115
military service in Great War;
    mentioned in dispatches 41-44, **41**,
    46, 95
differences with National Farmers'
    Union 44, 46-48
N.P.F.A. certificate presentation 113
Norfolk club chairman and president
    108

living in Cathedral Close, Norwich 112
physical fitness 27, 28, 77, 105, 118
playing for Cambridge University **4**, 17, **18**, 19-22, 26, 27
playing for Free Foresters 36-38, 54, 57, 60, 61-62, 68, 74-75, 78, 122
playing for the Gentlemen **32**, 35, **35**, 70
playing for Harrow 12, **13,** 14
playing for Norfolk, 1906-1908 8, 14, 17, **18**, 19; 1910-1914 22, **23**, 25-27, **29**, 31, 36
'all-round excellence' in 1920 59; 1921-1929 8, 61, 65, 67, 70, **76**, 77-82, **81**; 1930-1938 57, 58, 82, **85**, 86, 87, 89
'Indian Summer' with the bat; 1939 91, 92, **92**
'swan song' in 1946 105-107
partnership record for Gentlemen 71
partnership record for Norfolk 89
portrait by Oswald Birley 108
recovery from cancer 112
recruiting Jack Nichols as Norfolk's coach 61
school days at Cromer **11**, 12
school days at Harrow 12
singing at Horning meeting 67
social cricket in later life 5, 105, 106, 109-111, **110**, **111**
spectator at Lakenham in later life 6, 114
studying law at Cambridge University 17, 20, 21, 25
Test cricket 'possible' 64, 65, 115-122
tour of U.S.A. with Incogniti **32**, 33, 34, 123, 126
tributes from *Eastern Daily Press* and Sir Hubert Ashton 129, 130
unbeaten record against first-class touring sides 117, 118

Falcon, Michael, senior (father) 10, 41, 54, 92, 95, 96, 108
Falcon, Michael (grandfather) 10
Falcon, Michael (grandson) 97
Falcon, Michael Gascoigne (son) 12, 25, 34, 44, 56, 94, 96-98, 101,109, 114, 115, 127
Falcon, William (brother) 10, 15, 16, 41, 42
Falcon's XI 15, 90, 110, 111, **111**
Falcon and Birkbeck (land agents) 10
Falcon Brewery, Great Yarmouth 92, **93**
Falcon Cup competition 69

Falcon family name 10
Falcon House, Norwich 129, **129**
Falconer, Roderick **29**, 30, 35
Farnes, Kenneth 57
Faulkner, G.A. 62-65, **64**
R.T.Fellowes' XI 33
Fenner's Ground, Cambridge 17, 37, 78
Festival of Britain, 1951 110, **110**
Field, E.F. 27
Findlay, William 40, 100
Fitzwilliam Street, Cambridge 17, 20
The Fleggs, Norfolk 49
Fleming, M.V. 10
Folland, N.A. 124, 125
Foster, R.E. 38
Foster, F.R. 27, **32**, 119, 120
Foster, G.N. 62, **64**
Foster, H.K. 120
Fox, E.C.M. 12
Fox, James 12
France 42
Franklin, W.B. 74, 75, 80, 82-83, 89, 105, 116, 119
Free Foresters C.C. 8-9, 36-38, 54, 57, 60-62, 68, 74, 75, 78, 122
French, Lt-Col Hon E.G.F. 14
Frith, D.E.J. 40
Fry, C.B. 121, 122
Fulcher, E.J. **23**, **29**, 35

Gallipoli peninsula, Turkey 14, 42
Gascoigne, Capt. Charles (father-in-law) 54
Gascoigne, Kathleen (wife) 50, 54, 69, 78-79, **95**, 97, 98, 106, 112-114, 128
Gentlemen *v* Players matches 8, 22, 26, 27, **32**, 33, 35, **35**, 58-60, 68, 70, 71, 75, 78, 80, 117, 120, 123
Gentlemen of England XI 58
Gentlemen's XI 21
Germany 36, 46, 96, 104, 128
Gibson, C.H. 62-64, **64**, 119
Gibson, Ted **18**, **23**, **29**, 125
Gidea Park C.C., Romford 57
Gilligan, A.E.R. 71, 122
Glamorgan C.C.C. 35, 122
Golden Age of Norfolk Cricket, 1910-1914 24, 25
Golden Age of Norfolk Cricket, 1930s 82
Government, 1918-1922 45-47, 89
Government, 1922-1923 51-52
Grace, Dr W.G. 75
Gravesend, Kent 90
Great Norwich Flood, 1878 29

Great Yarmouth, Norfolk 49, 92, 93, **93**, 97, 102
Great Yarmouth C.C. 84
Great Yarmouth Water Works Co Ltd 93
Green, Sir John 47, 49
Greenway, C.E. 33
Gresham's School, Holt 109
Greswell, W.T. 37
Grierson, Henry 41
Gunn, George 59

Habgood, Anthony (great nephew) 16
Habgood, John (brother-in-law) 16
Habgood, John Michael (nephew) 16
Haifa, Palestine 43
Hammond, W.R. 68
Hampshire C.C.C. 101
Hancock, W.C. 29, 30
Hansard, report of parliamentary debates 50
Harbord, Sir Arthur, MP 102-103
Harris, Lord (fourth) 39
Harrison, George 112
Harrison, Peter 112, 115, 127
Harrow School 12, 15, 108
Harrow School eleven 12-15, **13**, 17, 79
Harrow Wanderers C.C. 14, 30, 123
Havering-atte-Bower, Essex 56, 57, 92
Hawke, Lord (seventh) 10, 21, 39,40, 60, 86
Headingley Cricket Ground, Leeds 121
Hearne, J.W. 100
Heaton, J.L. 86
Henderson, Fred 44, 45
Hendren, E.H. ('Patsy') 100
Hertford 91
Hertfordshire C.C.C. 36, 59, 65, 67, 68, 72, 74, 77-79, 82, 88-91, 105, 107, 124
Hewitt, George 48, 50, 52, 53
High Sheriff of Norfolk 12, 50, 55, 102, **102**
High Steward of Great Yarmouth 97
High Wycombe, Buckinghamshire 79
Hinckley, Leicestershire 81, 107
Hirst, G.H. 21
Hitch, J.W. 119, 120
Hoare, Captain V.R. 41
Hobbs, Sir John ('Jack') 59, 68, 70, 75, 128
Holdsworth, R.L. 61
Holkham Hall, Norfolk 101
Holmes, E.R.T. 37
Home Guard 101, **102**, 103
Honingham Cricket Week 33

Hooman, C.V.L. 22
Hordern, Dr H.V. 34
Horning and District C.C., Norfolk 67
Hornung, E.W. 84
Horstead, Norfolk 10, 55
Horstead Church 12, 96
Horstead House 10, **11**, 54, 94
Horstead Relief Fund 29
Horstead War Memorial 47
House of Commons 45, 46, 49-51, 53, 54, 56, 67, 121, 127, 129
House of Lords 53
Howard, Rupert 106
Howell, Harry 120
Hunstanton, Norfolk 70, 89, 106

Incogniti C.C. **32,** 32-34, 123
Indians, touring side 26, 66, 67, 117
Industrial Revolution 7
Inner Temple (Inn of Court) 25
Institution of Surveyors 10
Ireland 22, 33, 119
Ireland, J.F. 17, **18**, 20, 26, 27

Jackson, Rt Hon Sir Stanley, MP 40, 51, 86
Jackson, J.B. 103
Jardine, D.R. 37, 40, 60
Jarvis, L.K. 66
Jeeves, Percy 120
Jessop, G.L. **32**, 35, 112, 119
Jewson, P.W., MP 103, 106
Johnson, J.W. 70

Kent 8, 56
Kent C.C.C. 10, 21, 99, 106
Kent C.C.C. Second XI 61, 68, 74, 77, 79, 83, 84, 86-87, 89, 90
Kilner, Roy 59
King, J.B. 33, 34
King's Lynn, Norfolk 43
Knight, D.J. 58
Knox, N.A. 119

Labour Party 47, 48, 50, 52, 53
Lacon, E., and Co Ltd 92, **93**, 97, 102, 109, 113
Lacon, E.M. 92
Lakenham Cricket Ground, Norwich 5, 6, 14, 15, **23**, 27, 30, 36, 41, 66-68, 71, **72**, 74, 77, 80, 81, **81**, **85**, 86, 89, 96, 100, 104, 105, 107, 108, 110, **110**, 114, 127, 128
Lambert, April (daughter-in-law) 97
Lancashire C.C.C. 17, 62, 106, 120

Langdale, G.R. 104
Larwood, Harold 40
Lawton Smith, J.N. 124
LBW Law 87
Le Couteur, P.R. 22
Leicestershire C.C.C. 8, 26, 78, 107, 122
Leicestershire C.C.C. Second XI 73,
    79-81, 98
Leveson Gower, Sir Henry D.G. ('Shrimp')
    33, 39
H.D.G. Leveson Gower's XI 70
Levett, W.H.V. ('Hopper') 56
Liberal Party 43, 44, 47-53, 56, 89, 103,
    106
Lincolnshire C.C.C. 83, 84, 88-89, 124
Lingwood, Norfolk 99, 101
Lingwood, W.J. ('Jack') 84, **85**, 104
Lloyd George, Rt Hon Lord (British
    Prime Minister) 44
Loddon, Norfolk 50
London 40, 78
Lord's Cricket Ground 12, 13, 19, 33,
    38, 40, 58, 59, 89, 96, 100, 117
Lords and Commons XI 67
Low, H F. **76**, 80, **81**
Lowestoft, Suffolk 15
Lowry, T.C. 68
Lucas, C.E. 93
Lyttelton, Rev Hon Edward 55

Macartney, C.G. 63, 64, 130
MacLaren, A.C. 31, 33, 62-64, **64**, 71,
    116, 117, 120, 121, 130
A.C.MacLaren's XI, (Australia and New
    Zealand, 1922/23) 78
McDonald, E A. 63
Mace, A.F.A. 106, 107
Manchester Guardian newspaper 17, 19,
    21, 27, 58, 59, 63, 68, 71, 75
Mann, Sir Edward 20
Mann, F.George 110
F.G.Mann's XI 110, **110**
Mann, Frank T. 20, 25, 26, 39, 55, 93,
    94, 110, 115, 122
Manor Park, Horsford, Norfolk 108, **130**
Marriott, C.S. ('Father') 62, 75
Mary Falcon House, Burlingham 97-98
M.C.C. 19, 24, 26, 27, 30, 54, 58-60, 68,
    78, 79, 81, 86, 119
M.C.C. Committee 38-40, 66, 86, 87,
    100, 112
M.C.C. Cricket and Selection
    sub-Committee 39
M.C.C. Tennis and Rackets
    sub-Committee 39, 40

M.C.C. tour of Norfolk 28
Mason, J.R. 39
Mead, C.P. 27
Member of Parliament 51, 53, 54, 56,
    69, 89, 93, 121, 130
Meyer, R.J.O. ('Jack') 72, 78
Middlesex C.C.C. 8, 26, 55, 99, 100, 116,
    121
Middlesex C.C.C. Second XI 89
Mid-Norfolk C.C. 28
Miller, D.H. 124
Ministry of Health 49
Ministry of Information committee
    (Yarmouth) 103
Minor Counties Cricket Association 6,
    30, 35
Minor Counties Championship 12, 19,
    22, 24, 27, 28, 30, 31, 34, 38, 39, 56,
    58, 59, 61, 65, 66, 70, 77-80, 82, 84,
    86-91, 98-101, 104, 105, 106, 117,
    119, 121-125, 128
Minor Counties Championship
    Challenge Match 22, 23, 30, 31, 33,
    35, 66, 86, 87
Minor Counties XI 60, 61, 67, 71-73, **72**,
    75, **76**, 77, 118,121, 128
Minor Counties 'Team of the Century'
    123-125
Mohammad Nissar 71, **85**, 98
Mordy, Isabella (mother) 10, 16, 41, 54,
    96
Mordy, William (grandfather) 10
Mordy family name 10
Rev Morgan's XI 15
Munford, C.R. 124
Mynn, Alfred 56

Naples, Italy 103
National Debt 46
National Farmers' Union (N.F.U.) 44, 46,
    47, 48
National Government 103
National Playing Fields Association 113
National Seed Development
    Organisation 97
New, R.M. 124
New Zealanders, touring side 79-80, 84
Newnham College, Cambridge 96
Nichols, J.E. 61, 68, 73, **76**, 77, **81**, 82,
    85, 98, 106
Norfolk 7, 8, 10, 12, 16, 17, 28, 29, 37,
    40, 44-47, 51-58, 67, 69, 71, 75, 90,
    93, 94, 96-103, 106, 111,112, 116,
    128, 130

Norfolk Club and Ground XI 58, 90, 104, 106, 107
Norfolk County Council 47
Norfolk C.C.C. 5, 6, 8, 9, 12, 14, 15, **18**, 19-22, **23**, 24-31, **29**, 33-35, 38, 54, 58-61, 65-68, 70, 72-74, **76**, 77-81, **81**, 82-84, **85**, 86-91, 93, 98, 100, 101, 103-105, 107, 108, 110, 111, 114-119, 121, 123-126
Norfolk C.C.C. Committee 30, 103, 104, 126
Norfolk County Playing Fields Association 113
Norfolk (and Norwich) Cricket Association 60, 113
Norfolk Cricket Festival 58, 128
Norfolk crop rotation 7
Norfolk News newspaper 52-54, 78
Norfolk Territorial Forces Association 54
Norman England 7
Norman, Dr J.E. 30
North Walsham, Norfolk 44-45, 46
Northamptonshire C.C.C. 30, 66, 99, 122, 123
Northamptonshire Club and Ground XI 30
Northumberland C.C.C. 91
Norway 12, 103
Norwich 7, 29, 31, 49, 54, 68, 75, 84, 93, 98, 112
Norwich Prison 95
Norwich Repertory Company 84
'Norwich School' of painting 7
Norwich Union C.C. 90, 106, 110, 111
Norwich Union Fire and Life Insurance Societies 10, 12, 69, 92, 97, 102, 108, **108**, 109, 111, **111**
Norwich Wanderers C.C. 84, 87, 98 , 105, 118
Nottinghamshire C.C.C. Second XI 23
Nourse, A.W. ('Dave') 73
Nurton, M.D. 124, 125

Old Buckenham, Norfolk 31, 75, 116
Old Catton, Norfolk 46
Old Trafford Cricket Ground, Manchester 106, 121
The Oval Cricket Ground, Kennington 22, 35, **35**, 60, 68, 70, 71, 78, 80, 83, 117, 120
Overstrand C.C. 28, 89-90
Oxford University 82, 87, 96, 97
Oxford University C.C. 22, 27, 37, 38, 58, 60-62, 87, 122

Oxfordshire C.C.C. 124

Page, S.D. 41
Palairet, R.C.N. 40
Palestine 41-44, **41**, 95
Parfitt, P.H. 8
The Parks Cricket Ground, Oxford 61
Parliamentary Cricket Association 67
Patterson, W.H. 39
Pedder, G.R. 72, 141
Pegler, S.J. 31, 33
Pellew, C.E. ('Nip') 130
Pembroke College, Cambridge 15, 17, 20, 21
Pembroke College C.C. 17, 19
Penn, E.F. 41
Pennsylvania University C.C. 14
Percival, A.B. 124
Perkins, G.C. 124, 125
Philadelphia, United States 32-34
Pilch, D.G. 91, 111, **111**
Pilch, Fuller 8, 91
Pilch, G.E. 90, 91
G.E.Pilch's XI 110
Pilch, R.G. **29**, 91, 93
Plumb, S.G. 124, 125
Ponsford, W.H. 77
Popham, R.F. **29**, 31, 35
Powell, P.G. 111, **111**
Price, Sir Robert, MP 43
Prior, C.B.L. **23**, **29**, 29, 30, 58, 93, 104, 118

Radio Norfolk (B.B.C.) 8, 128
Radley, C.T. 8
Raedwald 7
Raikes, E.B. 41
Raikes, Rev G.B. 22, 23, **23**, 26, 27, **29**, 31, 59, 126
Reigate, Surrey 70
Repton School 10, 111
Reunert, Clive 13
Rhodes, Wilfred 27, 59
Roberts, H.E. 27
Robinson, Emmott 70
Robinson, L.G. 31, 116
Lionel Robinson's XI 31, 35, 75
Rogers, C.J. 91
Romford, Essex 56, 57
Root, C.F. 79
Rought-Rought family 83, 107
Rought-Rought, Basil W. **76**, **81**, **85**, 101, 103
Rought-Rought, Rodney C. **76**, 80, 81, **81**, 91, 104, 125

Royal Agricultural College, Cirencester 10
Royal Air Force 128
Royal Engineers 42
Royal Field Artillery **41**, 42
Royal Forestry Society 97
Royal Norfolk Regimental Museum 42
Ryder, 'Jack' 77, 130

Saggers, M.J. 8
St Augustine's Lodge, Ditchingham 106
St Hilda's College, Oxford 97
St James' Church, Pockthorpe 6
St John Ambulance 97
St Paul's Church, Knightsbridge 54
Sanders, Sir Robert, MP (later Lord Bayford) 47
Sandham, Andrew 70
Saxon England 7
Scarborough, Yorkshire 26, 27, 78, 119
Scotland 12, 83
Sedgeford School 106
Seely, Sir Hugh, MP (later Lord Sherwood) 47-53
Sewell, E.H.D. 14, 28
Sheffield, Yorkshire 86
Shilleto, Rev A. 91
Shore, Charles 84
Simms, H.L. 31, **32**
Simons, Robert 124
Slade School of Art, London 97
Smith, E.W. ('Billy') 125
Somerset C.C.C. 64, 72, 104, 126
South Africa 12, 62, 97, 120
South Africans, touring side 28, 31, 67, 70-73, **72**, 81, **81**, 99, 117, 118, 121
Spooner, R.H. 120
Sprowston Hall. Norwich 10, 96
Staffordshire C.C.C. 26, 29, 36, 61, 65, 70, 74, 82, 86, 105, 116, 121, 124
Stainburn, Cumberland 10
Stevens, B.G.W. 114
Stevens, G.A. **18**, 22, **23**, 28, **29**, 69, 72, 73, 75, **76**, **81**, 82, 126
Stoke-on-Trent, Staffordshire 26, 30
Stokes, D.W. ('Bill') 124
Strudwick, Herbert 71
Strauss, E.A., MP 56
Suffield Park School, Cromer **11**, 12
Suffolk 7
Suffolk C.C.C. 30, 124
Surrey C.C.C. 8, 19, 27
Surrey C.C.C. Second XI 60, 70, 80, 83, 84, 124
Sussex 101

Sussex C.C.C. 8, 17, 19, 20, 26, 27, 93
Sutcliffe, Herbert 59
Sutton, J.Arthur 124, 125
Swanton, E.W. ('Jim') **110**, 127
Tarrant, F.A. 31
Tate, F.W. 27
Tate, M.W. 118
Taylor, H.W. 73, **81**
Taylor, W.B 44, 45
Tennyson, Lord (third) 121, 122, 128
Test cricket 8, 9, 14, 28, 33, 34, 39, 57, 62-64, 71, 72, 87, 90, 91, 100, 112, 114-122, 126, 128
Thelveton, Norfolk 20
Theobald, H.E. **85**, 91, 105
Thetford Heath, Norfolk 101
Thompson, G.J. 123, 125
Thompson, W.S. 88, 107, 111, **111**
Thorne, G.C. 103
C.I.Thornton's XI 59
Thurgar, R.W. 15, **23**, **29**, 41
The Times newspaper 19-22, 27, 30, 58, 61, 63, 71, 75, 80, 119
Titchmarsh, C.H. 72, 73, 77, 78, 82, 124, 125
Tobruk, Libya 16
Transport Corps 42
Trevor, Col P.C.W. 70
Trondheim, Norway 103
Tyldesley, J.T. 27

Ullswater, Lord 39

Varsity Match 19, 20, 22, 27
Vikings 7
Voce, William 40

Waddington, Abram 120
Walker, D.F. 8, 34, 83, **85**, 87, 91, 103, 104
War, First World (Great) 8, 14, 15, 24, 25, 39, 41-43, **41**, 56, 58, 61, 79, 82, 87, 95, 101,105, 119, 120, 123, 130
War, Second World 8, 41, 66, 67, 83, 96, 101-103, 105-107, 123
Warner, Sir Pelham ('Plum') 26, 34, 39, 40, 43, 70, 71, 112, 115, 118, 120'
P.F.Warner's XI 58
Warwickshire C.C.C. 120
Washbrook, Cyril 122
Watson, Harold 59, 60, 72, 73, 82
Watson, Vera 60
Webb, A.J. 124
Webster, Very Rev Alan 114

West Indians, touring side 8, 14, 68, 80, 81, 92
West Norfolk 106, 107
Western Australia, University of 22
Westminster School 67
Whitbread and Co Ltd 16, 97
Whysall, W.W. ('Dodge') 68
Wickham, Rev A.P. 126
Wilson, B.K. **23**, 100
Wiltshire 54
Wiltshire C.C.C. 86
Wisden Cricketers' Almanack 17, 59, 75, 77, 79, 86, 116, 117, 126
Witham, Essex 15
Wood, George E.C. 62, **64**
Wood, George H. 125

Wood, B.John 83, 101, 103
Woodfull, W.M. 77
Worcestershire C.C.C. 61, 79, 122
Workington, Cumberland 10
Wright, C.C.G. **18**, 19
Wright, J.F. 47, 48
Wroxham, Norfolk 44
Wuffinga dynasty 7

Yarmouth C.C. 106
Yarmouth and District C.C. 28
Yaxley, Philip 126
Yorkshire 60, 86
Yorkshire C.C.C. 19, 21, 30, 59, 119, 120
Yorkshire C.C.C. Second XI 86
Y.M.C.A. 75